C L A S S I C
CRACKER

CLASSIC
CRACKER

FLORIDA'S WOOD-FRAME VERNACULAR ARCHITECTURE

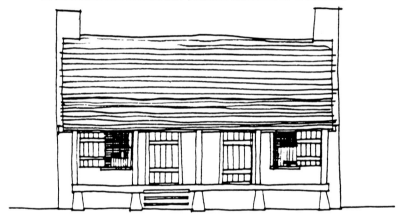

RONALD W. HAASE

PINEAPPLE PRESS
SARASOTA, FLORIDA

Inquires should be addressed to:
Pineapple Press, Inc.
P.O. Drawer 16008
Southside Station
Sarasota, Florida 34239

LIBRARY OF CONGRESS
CATALOGING-IN-PUBLICATION
DATA
Haase, Ronald W.
     Classic cracker : Florida's wood-frame
vernacular architecture / Ronald W. Haase,
-- 1st ed.
          p.   cm.
     ISBN   1-56164-013-1
     1. Wooden-frame buildings--Florida. 2.
Vernacular architecture--Florida.   I. Title.
NA730.F6H2   1992
728'.37'09759--dc20   92-10189
                                        CIP

Design by Steve Duckett
Typography by Millicent Hampton-Shepherd

Printed in Hong Kong

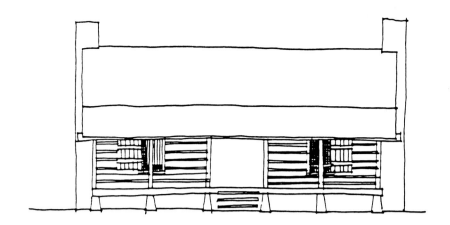

CONTENTS

ACKNOWLEDGMENTS

This work enjoyed the help of many supporters. It is important that appreciation be shown to the National Endowment for the Arts for funding the initial research conducted in preparing the text and gathering the images presented here. The University of Florida provided sabbatical leave permitting me to draw loose ends together into this volume.

A number of librarians helped me to sort through historic documents, making many useful suggestions along the way. The first of these was Ms. Ann Weaver, now retired from the Architecture and Fine Arts Library at the University of Florida. The staff at the University of Florida's P.K. Yonge Library of Florida History was of great assistance to me as was Joan P. Morris at the Florida Photographic Collection of the State Archives in Tallahassee.

Acknowledgment also is given to the many students in the College of Architecture at the University of Florida who have studied the Cracker ways of building with me, especially those who are convinced, as I am, that "vernacular" is a term full of life and contemporary meaning.

My daughter, Jennifer, helped me to explore and appreciate Henry Glassie's many works on folk architecture and I have drawn copiously from them. George Gillespie assisted by tracking down examples of contemporary houses which draw upon traditional vernacular imagery.

Donna Jenkins, a friend and journalist, offered invaluable advice on structure and format, and two tireless ladies, Deborah Robinson and Tammy Johns, helped produce the typed manuscript.

Finally, my wife, Janet, has continuously inspired, cajoled, nudged and faithfully supported this work through the far too many years it took to produce it. I dedicate it to her with respect and love.

Ronald W. Haase

FOREWORD

For the pioneers who ventured through the woods or down streams and rivers to settle here, Florida must have seemed a formidable — and amazing — place. I often marvel at the life that these settlers led, in such close concert with the land, with such simple satisfactions. In an era of car phones and fax machines, it all seems distant enough to have been another epoch, not simply a century or less ago.

In *Classic Cracker*, Ron Haase has captured not just an architectural style but an unsung piece of our past, and it is a compelling story. It is his own story, in a way, because he came to know and cherish the Cracker house as an outsider at first, but in the quest to learn about it, he found, literally as well as figuratively, a home.

Cracker architecture is, of course, a worthy and really quite beautiful vernacular style on its own, but there is more to it. I love the quote from the Roman writer Juvenal that goes, "never does nature say one thing and wisdom another," because it is profound and true, even in architecture, the art in which man tames the elements. In Florida, it is the Cracker house that has most mediated between the manmade and the natural.

Over the years, we've lost that primal quality in so much of our architecture, the beauty that comes when architecture does exactly what it's supposed to do — provide us shelter, keep us warm in winter and cool in summer, protect us from the sun and the rain. That's integrity, real authenticity, and it doesn't exist in far too much of our architecture today.

Beth Dunlop
Architecture Critic
Miami Herald

The hammock lightened with the stir of morning. Blue smoke from a fatwood fire curled from the chimney of the house. It spread in a canopy under the live oaks and magnolias. The vast branches formed an impenetrable roof over the floor of the forest, and the smoke eddied back on itself, smothering the low dwelling. For an instant there was no evidence that human life was here or ever had been. There was only hammock, black with its own shadows, damp with its own sunlessness. The morning vapor, blending with the smoke, was prehistoric. The dense vegetation was ageless, indifferent to mortal contact.

From *Golden Apples*
by MARJORIE KINNAN RAWLINGS

**Old Cracker homestead
on Hwy. 27 near Fenhal-
loway, Taylor County.**

THE CRACKER ARCHITECTURE
OF FLORIDA

O ne of the most welcome phenomena in contemporary architectural design and criticism

is the renewed interest in history as a legitimate design influence. With the advent of the Modern

Movement earlier in this century, history was rejected as a form-making determinant by

advocates of a "new spirit" in architecture. The International Style that emerged had technology

and functionalism as its theoretical base. Ignoring precedent, each new design evolved from a

critical analysis of programmatic needs tempered by the lean abstraction of a reductivist attitude

toward building technology. Author and social critic Tom Wolfe called it "starting from zero" in

his popular treatise *From Bauhaus to Our House.*

After sixty years of this clean-slate approach to design, however, many in the architectural

profession have tired of the starkness of their creations. A large number of contemporary designers have cast off the monk's robes of the International Style and sought more richness and meaning in the built environment. As if through a rear-view mirror, historic form, typology and precedent once more have been seen as a base to build upon. Emotional content, so long cleaned away from the smooth white boxes of Modernism, is being given its due attention in design. Unfortunately, in a rush to add depth and meaning to a new post-modern architecture, much that is inappropriate and ineffectual is being borrowed from history and applied without concern for context to many an elevation or building plan.

Concern for this lack of discrimination in post-modern historic allusions has led some architects to a more accurate and detailed study of regional tradition. Given a clearer understanding of the historic architectural forms around us, we might envision new designs that build appropriately on the same forces of nature, regional culture and available technology that originally gave shape to our architectural heritage.

As we look at regional history, however, it is difficult to identify the exact boundaries that define a particular vernacular. Some drift across many states. The New England saltbox, for instance, is comfortable in New Jersey as well as Nova Scotia. In like manner, the Southwestern adobe ranch house seems to suit both southern California and western Texas. The appropriateness of each of these regional architectural phenomena has been well documented and the library resources available to designers in those states and provinces are at their fingertips.

One peculiar omission seems to exist in our regional architectural library. It is the volume that would be labeled "The Cracker Architecture of Florida." This work attempts to fill that void and to supply architects, historians and the interested public with documentation on the typological development of this most special and quickly disappearing segment of our architectural heritage.

As we begin, the term "Cracker" should be defined. Originating in nearby southern Georgia, Cracker came into use to designate the backwoods country folk who cracked their corn to make meal, a staple in their diet that was used for everything from corn pone to corn fritters and to the most delicious of all pan foods, "hush puppies," fried right in the same gritty fat as the day's catch. North Florida's early settlers inherited this identity as "corn crackers" but they personalized the meaning of the word. It became a reference to the sharp, loud crack of the leather whips used to drive cattle or inspire a tired mule to pull harder on the plow.

Today, Cracker refers to the unpretentious people and architecture found on farms and in rural communities still sprinkled throughout these peninsular and panhandle wetlands. Their simple grace and beauty deserve to be chronicled, but, alas, more exciting times and more dashing people have figured all too prominently in the written history of Florida. We know of the Spanish at early St. Augustine, for instance, and the builders of those spectacular Moorish domes and arches of boom-time hotels in Tampa and Palm Beach. Add the swashbuckling pirates, rum-runners and wreckers who constructed the breezy Bahama-styled houses of Key West. All these historic builders and their buildings have been duly honored and described. But the truly fundamental regional architecture of the Florida Cracker has never been championed.

Yet the charm of Cracker times and ways has inspired such writers as Marjorie Kinnan Rawlings, whose books, *The Yearling* and *Cross Creek,* attracted many of us to search out North Florida's enchantment. My own work as an architect and a teacher has been strongly influenced by her words.

Recognizing that the time is long overdue for a definitive work on the Cracker architecture of Florida, I am offering this book as a contribution toward that goal. It is perceived as an opportunity to breathe life into the vernacular typology of Cracker farmhouse, townhouse and plantation and to illustrate ways by which that vernacular may serve as paradigm for contemporary architecture. The time frame starts with the first homesteaders of early 19th-century Florida and continues through the Seminole Indian Wars, the Civil War, and on into the first decades of the 20th century when boom-time invasions of outsiders distort the isolated regional peculiarities of Cracker life.

Before the reader continues, another term of considerable importance needs to be defined. The term is "vernacular." For many this word applies to things of the distant past, dead and gone and interesting only as seen through the dusty perspective of history. As used here, however, vernacular refers to "the native language or dialect of a particular region or place." This identification with "linguistic" vernacular gives life and energy and contemporary qualities to all things vernacular. From this point of view the "visual" language of Cracker Florida remains vital and as much alive today as it was nearly two hundred years ago.

The flutter-mill was at work. It turned with the easy rhythm of the great water-mill at Lynne that ground corn into meal.

Jody drew a deep breath. He threw himself on the weedy sand close to the water and abandoned himself to the magic of motion. Up, over, down, up, over, down — the flutter-mill was enchanting. The bubbling spring would rise forever from the earth, the thin current was endless. The spring was the beginning of waters sliding to the sea. Unless leaves fell, or squirrels cut sweet bay twigs to drop and block the fragile wheel, the flutter-mill might turn forever. When he was an old man, as old as his father, there seemed no reason why this rippling movement might not continue as he had begun it.

From *The Yearling*
by MARJORIE KINNAN RAWLINGS

Old Cracker homestead
on country road near
Williston, Levy County.

CHAPTER ONE

A PERSONAL SEARCH
FOR CRACKER FLORIDA

I n the summer of 1977, my family and I left a brooding Victorian house on a hillside overlooking

Littleton, New Hampshire, and headed south for Gainesville, Florida. New job, new friends, new

home. After loading a U-Haul truck with all our belongings (minus an ancient black cat that got to fly

Eastern), we aimed the truck toward I-95 southbound.

To psych ourselves up for a major shift in climate, geography and lifestyle, we took turns

reading aloud from Marjorie Kinnan Rawlings' classic Cracker novel, *The Yearling*. I hoped that

the kids would identify with Jody in the novel and imitate his innate curiosity for exploring the

North Florida backwoods and wetlands. For myself, I was anxious to find inspiration for new

architectural imagery. I needed to shift my visual thinking from snug, shingled New England

boxes to open screened porches and wide shady verandas. Janet, my wife, is a weaver and she was

Marjorie Kinnan
Rawlings' home in Cross
Creek, Alachua County.

was looking forward to shedding heavy hand-made woolen shawls and wall hangings in ex-change for lightweight cotton textiles and tapestries.

Upon arrival in Florida, we settled into a little rented red brick house within walking dis-tance to my new office on the campus of the Uni-versity of Florida, where I would be a professor in the College of Architecture. I had a week or two before reporting in, so, after resettling all our be-longings, we put on our shorts, opened all the jalousie windows, turned on the attic fan and went out into the street to meet the neighbors.

Well … it was August, and this late summer season brought with it the first disappointment in our anticipated love affair with Florida. There wasn't a soul to be seen. No kids playing stickball in the street; no mothers gossiping from porch to porch; no good ol' boys hunkerin' in the dirt and swappin' yarns. Where was the Florida of our great expectations?

A week or so later we finally did get to see the neighbors. We found them sneaking out the side doors of their air-conditioned houses, into their air-conditioned cars, and slipping off to air-

conditioned supermarkets and shopping centers. What a disillusion!

Not to be totally discouraged, I set out every weekend with my camera, scouring the country-side for the Florida Cracker homesteads, farm-houses and lifestyles that I knew were out there somewhere. What I found were dilapidated shacks, ignored by time and their former occu-pants. Beautiful still, but weather-beaten and bio-degrading in the relentless Florida climate. As I photographed the old homesteads, my imagina-tion began to conjure up fanciful images of fathers and sons working together to construct houseforms molded by tradition and hand-crafted with skills taught by one generation to another. In many cases what I found, however, was the house of someone's Cracker grandparents sitting vacant and collapsing in a front yard while out back sat the new "manufactured housing" of their "redneck" offspring.

As a new professor at the University of Florida, I was granted some "seed money" that first year to explore the energy-related concepts of how well the North Florida vernacular farmhouse

**Old Cracker homestead
with mobile home out
back near McIntosh,
Marion County.**

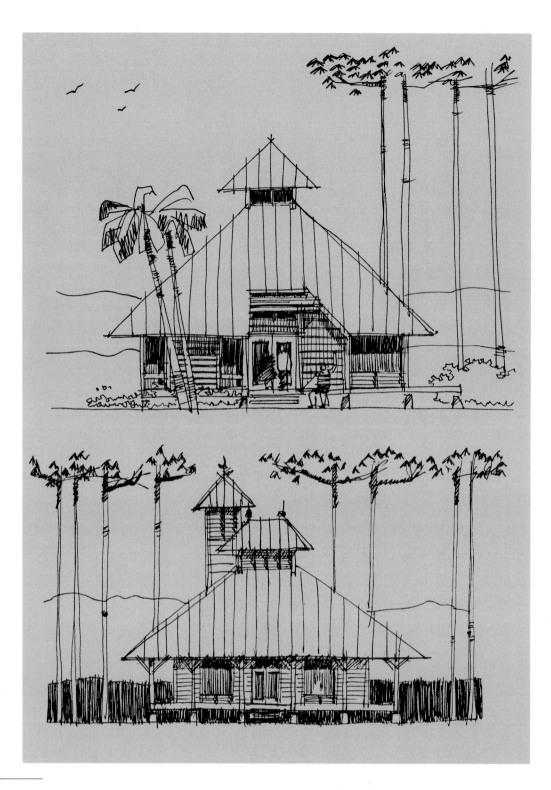

Lazy Sunday afternoon "doodlings" by the author.

was adapted to its subtropical setting. The passive technological attitudes that living close to nature required of any true Cracker or transplanted New England carpetbagger filled my teaching and my work. Devising ways to augment shade and air movement became the fundamentals of a new religion for me. Living without air conditioning and learning to actually enjoy high humidity were new badges of courage that my whole family wore proudly. I lectured and cajoled at any energy conservation workshop or ladies' auxiliary luncheon that would have me, flashing slide after slide of tin-roofed, raised-platformed Cracker allusions until we all nearly wept with shared enthusiasm.

Lake House designed by the author. Winner of Award from American Solar Energy Society in 1982.

My architectural sketches and doodlings from those first years in Florida took what I saw as the architectural elements of Cracker farmhouses and combined them into an eclectic storehouse of images that I called up from time to time. They served as a ready resource for my residential design work which became an amalgam of Victorian-like compositions but with austere detailing and L-shaped verandas topped by an assembly of towers and belvederes.

Encouraged by a few awards for my Crackeresque designs, I applied to the National Endowment for the Arts for funding to write a book on the subject. My proposal was successful and read in part: "The time is long overdue for the definitive treatise on the Cracker architecture of Florida."

With the research, travel and photography for my book now complete, I have been struck by a sharp sense of the classic qualities of Cracker architecture. The terminology and typology were familiar to me — single-pens, dog-trots, four-square Georgian plans. But it wasn't until I trekked from Pensacola to Key West and from Micanopy to Marianna, visiting house after house, that a pattern of significance began to appear. Before that time I had seen too many picturesque Victorians and asymmetrical saltboxes to catch on to the purity of form in the basic Cracker farmhouse. I had not isolated in my mind's eye the

Modest farmhouse on Hwy. 27 with porch partially filled in, Lafayette County.

initial symmetry and classic simplicity that each Cracker farmhouse began with. My vision was obscured by the vagaries of a porch half filled in to add a bedroom, or a shed added to provide needed storage, or the sophistication of an indoor toilet. With time, the closing in of an open dog-trot and other such compositional adjustments had nullified in my mind the initial classic clarity of these forms.

Now I looked closer, peeling back time to find the bare essentials, the basic beginnings, the fundamental form that a son had constructed in reaction to the tradition of his father's house.

It is appropriate to identify the guiding light whose scholarly research led me, vicariously, through my own search for the Cracker roots of vernacular architecture in North Florida. That person is the noted cultural geographer, Henry

Glassie, whose important work, *Pattern in the Material Folk Culture of the Eastern United States*, has inspired me and dozens of my architectural students over the past decade. Glassie outlines for us the many stages in the evolution of the Southern rural houseform but he touches little, if at all, on the role of Cracker Florida in this emerging pattern.

What this work of mine attempts to do, then, is to review Glassie's typological outline with emphasis on an illustration of the vernacular architecture of the early settlers of North Florida. The exciting adventure for me has been searching out a very special architectural amalgam: the classic principles of rational form-making blended with the truly regional integrity of North Florida vernacular that is embodied in that most modest of forms, the Cracker farmhouse.

As an orientation for the reader to more detailed explanations in the chapters which follow, an outline of the evolutionary typology of Cracker architecture is set out in the next few pages.

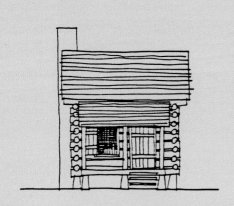

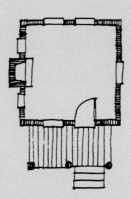

SINGLE-PEN

With nearly universal consistency, the single-room or single-pen house is the first construction effort of any pioneering home-steader. Using the basic materials and skills at hand, these simple shelters are built of logs, quickly and without the benefit of romanticized detail or decoration. A special feature of the single-pen log house in Florida, however, was the incorporation of a broad shady porch. The hot and humid climate of the region demanded it.

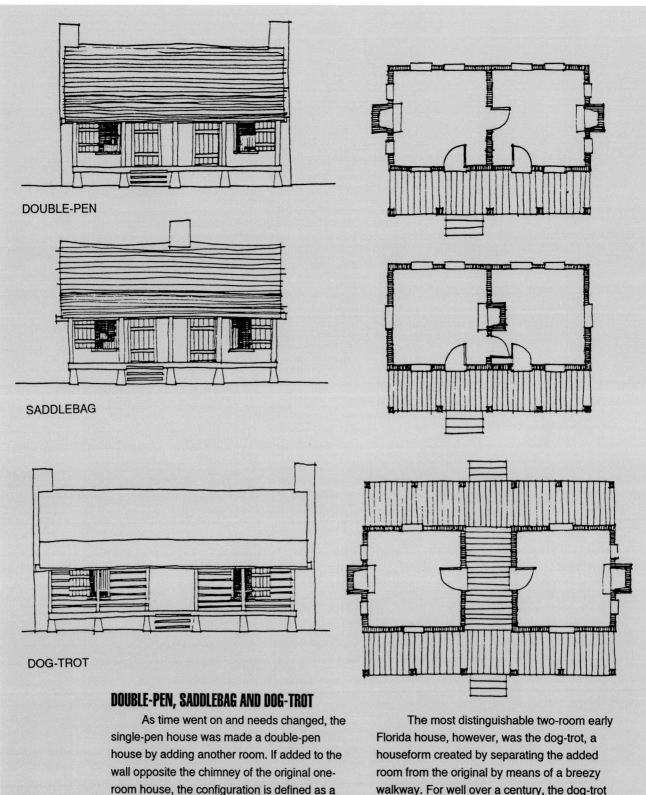

DOUBLE-PEN

SADDLEBAG

DOG-TROT

DOUBLE-PEN, SADDLEBAG AND DOG-TROT

As time went on and needs changed, the single-pen house was made a double-pen house by adding another room. If added to the wall opposite the chimney of the original one-room house, the configuration is defined as a double-pen house. Other times the addition was made against the wall containing the chimney and this would be a saddlebag house.

The most distinguishable two-room early Florida house, however, was the dog-trot, a houseform created by separating the added room from the original by means of a breezy walkway. For well over a century, the dog-trot houseform has been the dominant image, in most people's minds, representing Florida Cracker architecture.

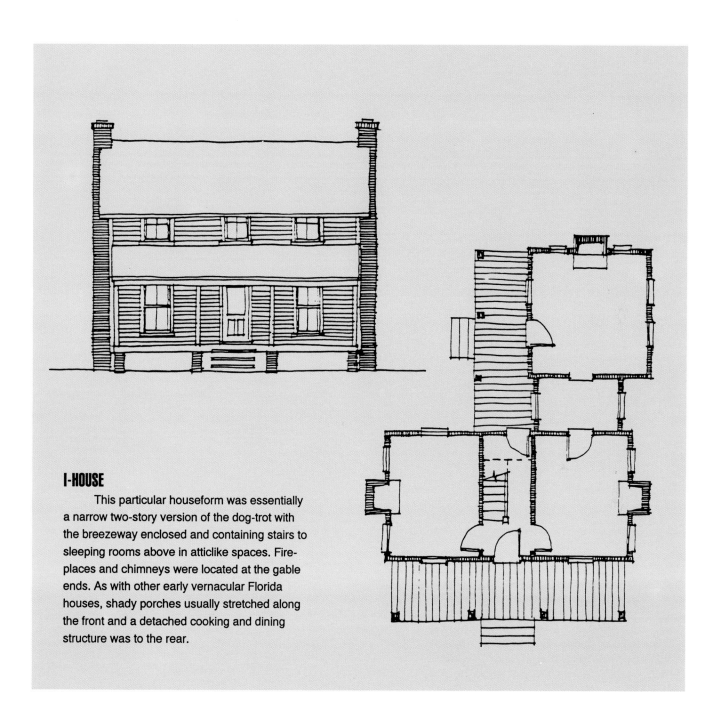

I-HOUSE

This particular houseform was essentially a narrow two-story version of the dog-trot with the breezeway enclosed and containing stairs to sleeping rooms above in atticlike spaces. Fireplaces and chimneys were located at the gable ends. As with other early vernacular Florida houses, shady porches usually stretched along the front and a detached cooking and dining structure was to the rear.

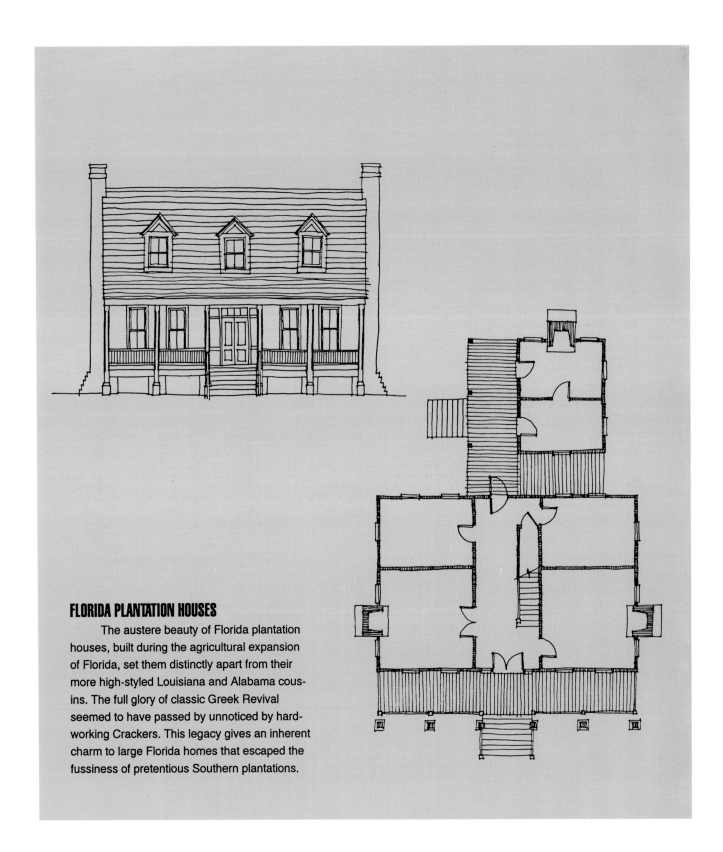

FLORIDA PLANTATION HOUSES

The austere beauty of Florida plantation houses, built during the agricultural expansion of Florida, set them distinctly apart from their more high-styled Louisiana and Alabama cousins. The full glory of classic Greek Revival seemed to have passed by unnoticed by hardworking Crackers. This legacy gives an inherent charm to large Florida homes that escaped the fussiness of pretentious Southern plantations.

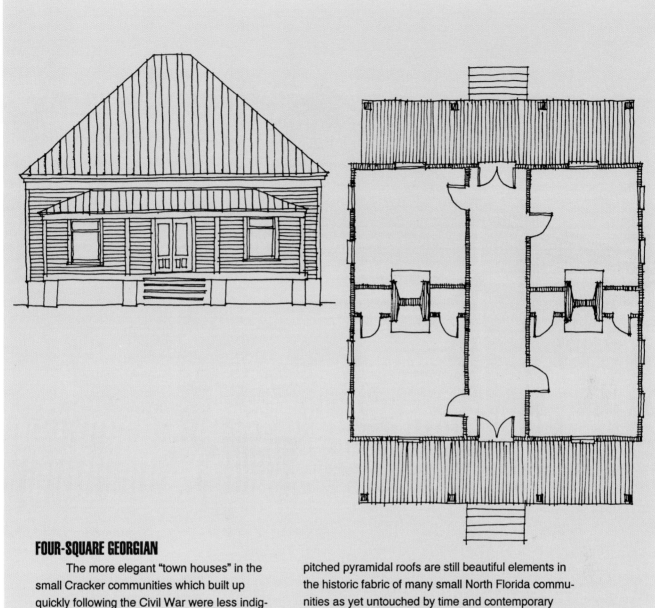

FOUR-SQUARE GEORGIAN

The more elegant "town houses" in the small Cracker communities which built up quickly following the Civil War were less indigenously derived, more self-conscious in design, and followed the four-square Georgian plan popular in sophisticated urban centers to the north. Their double chimneys and steeply pitched pyramidal roofs are still beautiful elements in the historic fabric of many small North Florida communities as yet untouched by time and contemporary development. Their broad porches alone set them apart from architectural imagery which could be found from Bangor, Maine, to Melrose, Florida, in the late 19th century.

As Greek Revival pretentions and the gaudiness of Victorian decorative styles eventually descended upon North Florida, they marked an end to vernacular imagery for the Crackers. Such outside influences and international attitudes had a tendency to water down regional qualities in speech, lifestyle and general outlook as well as in architectural expression. This cultural dilution, coupled with an economical access to air conditioning, eventually all but wiped out Florida's Cracker architectural heritage.

The Florida scrub was unique. The man Lantry recognised its quality as well as its remoteness. There was perhaps no similar region anywhere. It was a vast dry rectangular plateau, bounded on three sides by two rivers. The Ocklawaha, flowing towards the north, bounded it on the west. At the north-west corner of the rectangle the Ocklawaha turned sharply at right angles and flowed due east, joining, at the north-east corner, the St. John's River which formed the eastern demarcation.

Within these deep watery lines the scrub stood aloof, uninhabited through its wider reaches. The growth repelled all human living. The soil was a tawny sand, from whose parched infertility there reared, indifferent to water, so dense a growth of scrub pine — the Southern spruce — that the effect of the massed thin trunks was of a limitless, canopied stockade. It seemed impenetrable, for a man-high growth of scrub oak, myrtle, sparkleberry and ti-ti filled the interstices. Wide areas, indeed, admitted of no human passage.

From *South Moon Under*
by MARJORIE KINNAN RAWLINGS

19th-century single-pen house at the Tallahassee Junior Museum, Leon County. (Photo by Dan Branch)

CHAPTER TWO

A SINGLE-PEN HOMESTEAD FOR STARTERS

In the early 1800s during the second Spanish occupation of Florida, the scattered homesteads of pioneer settlers in North Central Florida were few and far between. The population in the coastal communities of St. Augustine, St. Marks and Pensacola barely added up to one thousand souls, and life in the interior of this frontier peninsula was rugged and demanding. It appealed to renegades and runaways, offering an isolated hideaway for them. More respectable pioneers in the expanding young nation elected to move to the west, attracted by the easy navigation of the Mississippi and the wide open spaces of the newly acquired Louisiana territories beyond.

The rough and tumble Florida pioneer did not arrive in well organized and guided communal wagon trains. He had to search out, on his own, poorly defined trails into the dense forests and occasionally encountered impenetrable wetlands. No cleared roads or freshly cut railway right-of-ways assisted his movements south across the Georgia border. I imagine a gaunt, sallow-faced man, a long leather thong whip in one hand and a shot gun lethargically dangling from the other, trudging alongside an equally tired old mule pulling a wooden cart with all the man's earthly belongings. If any woman could tolerate the companionship of such a dreary soul, I see her carrying a load of lashed-together household goods and young-uns nearly equal in weight to that which the beast is pulling.

We might imagine the progress of such lonely outcasts from some slightly more hospitable environment to the north and see how they built on these forlorn beginnings as they sought to carve out a new life in the Florida scrub, a new life that was forced upon them by some lawless act or self-elected as a retreat from crowding social contact; either way this was a journey born out of bitterness, stubbornness, or both.

The first-generation Florida Cracker was not a pillar of society. A life of hard knocks had not been a bad school, however, for it had taught both man and woman the skills they needed and given them the determination that was required to survive in this new life. They had the sense to pick some high, dry piece of land to set their homestead upon, finding a sandy "island" in the scrub that wouldn't flood with every cloudburst. There they would begin to clear a little circle of land to build their first crude house. Tall straight pines were felled, cut into logs and notched to interlock at their ends. These were raised, one atop another, to form the walls of a single room that would provide shelter and a centering place to this small pioneer family for the first few years of their bleak existence in this strange new environment. Since shelter was required quickly, the logs were probably left round with only the bark and spongy outer growth peeled off. These would have been placed on a few low flat stones for a foundation and packed around with sand at the base. The same sand would have served as a floor. If the spring weather was mild and time allowed, the first round of logs would have been set high off the damp ground on wedge-shaped piers of heart pine or cypress and a raised floor of thick planking or split logs laid down.

The top logs of two opposite walls would cantilever out to support steeply sloping log rafters, thus forming a gabled roof end. Smaller diameter logs or purlins were spiked or pegged perpendicular to the rafters and parallel to the ridge line. Until roofing shingles could be rived from short, round logs of cedar or cypress, palm fronds lashed to the purlins would temporarily cover the house and direct the rain off the roof.

Finally, the cracks between logs were chinked with moist clay and a never-ending maintenance cycle began. Windows may have been small in this first crude house and covered over with woven fabric to help keep out insects and the elements. Exterior shutters attached by rough iron hinges might have followed in the days ahead as well as a plank door with a wooden latch.

Shady porches front and back (all around, if time and helpful hands were abundant) were perhaps the major distinction between this single-pen Cracker cabin and the "primitive hut" which French abbé Marc-Antoine Laugier evokes for us in his *Essay on Architecture*, 1753. Laugier's simple hut was laden with symbolic meaning about house and shelter.

A century later and without the benefit of intellectual discourse with Laugier, the equally modest Seminole Indian "chickee" came into being as a houseform with a manifest suitability to Florida's hot and humid climate.

Laugier's primitive hut, from the frontispiece to the 2nd edition of his *Essay on Architecture*.

"Let us look at man in his primitive estate without any aid or guidance other than his natural instincts. . . . He wants to make himself a dwelling that protects but does not bury him. Some fallen branches in the forest are the right material for his purpose; he chooses four of the strongest, raises them upright and arranges them in a square; across their top he lays four other branches; on these he hoists from two sides yet another row of branches which, inclining towards each other, meet at their highest point. He then covers this kind of roof with leaves so closely packed that neither sun nor rain can penetrate. Thus, man is housed."

From "Essay On Architecture," 1753
by MARC-ANTOINE LAUGIER

SEMINOLE CHICKEE

The Seminole was a runaway, on the move, pursued relentlessly into a lifestyle that involved constant disruption. The migratory camp of four or five chickees ringed around an open cook shed could be built in less than a week. The Indians' simple construction technique and the frugal investment in time and materials made it less difficult to abandon when necessary to move deeper into the swamp as white soldiers got closer.

Each family shelter, or chickee, was about 10 feet by 20 feet in plan with a single elevated platform set three feet off the wet ground. Upright posts were built of palmetto or cypress logs as available. Pounded into the ground for anchorage, the top of each post was set at about seven feet high and then notched to receive a horizontal log girder. To this, sloping rafters of lighter poles were lashed with rope made of palmetto fibers. Center poles at the short ends of the house held a higher ridge beam.

Once the rafter poles were in place, smaller purlin poles were placed to bridge across them and layers of palm frond thatch were tied to them. The thatching hung low out over the structural frame so that ample shade and rain protection were provided for the sleeping and dining space it sheltered.

Pole beams set on short posts held the single platform which was decked with split palmetto logs, flat side up. Occasionally, with a false sense of security and permanence, a Seminole family might add two or three more such open and shady shelters permitting each to be used separately for either sleeping or dining. Ultimately, however, the need to move on would force the abandonment of such comforts.

The McNair/Black House at the Tallahassee Junior Museum, a single-pen pioneer structure built of hand-hewn pine logs. Originally constructed in the 1870s in Liberty County, the house was moved to the Junior Museum in 1961.

Some early white settlers emulated the open chickee of the Seminole for their first constructed shelter or built even more primitive lean-tos covered with palm fronds. Most, however, built log houses from the pine trees felled to clear their new farming land. The simple beauty of a modest, yet elegant, first Cracker homestead is wonderfully preserved for us at the Junior Museum in Tallahassee. While providing only a modicum of shelter for the pioneering family, this particular single-pen house was obviously constructed by craftsmen with a discerning and innate sense of proportion.

Here, the singular room for living is a rectangle roughly 15 feet wide and 20 feet long. A-10-foot-wide porch extends around three sides of the house with a doorway in each of these three sides. The gable-ended fourth side is where a marvelous stick-and-mud chimney stands, serving the clay-lined fireplace that provided sufficient warmth during Florida's mild winters and a place to cook

the pioneer family's meals. Later, as with most early vernacular homesteads throughout the southeast, a separate kitchen structure was built out back to isolate the heat of cooking and the hazards of fire.

The gable end opposite the fireplace in this single-pen house extends boldly out over the west porch. A horizontal tie beam keeps the eaves from spreading outward under the roof load.

The tranquil setting encountered at the Junior Museum belies a bit the cantankerous, loner qualities of early Cracker homesteaders. The hard labor of seeking out an existence in the Florida scrub may have dried up whatever sociability these tobacco-chewing, snuff-snorting farmers possessed. Every account of travelers and naturalists that explored the sandy peninsula in the 19th

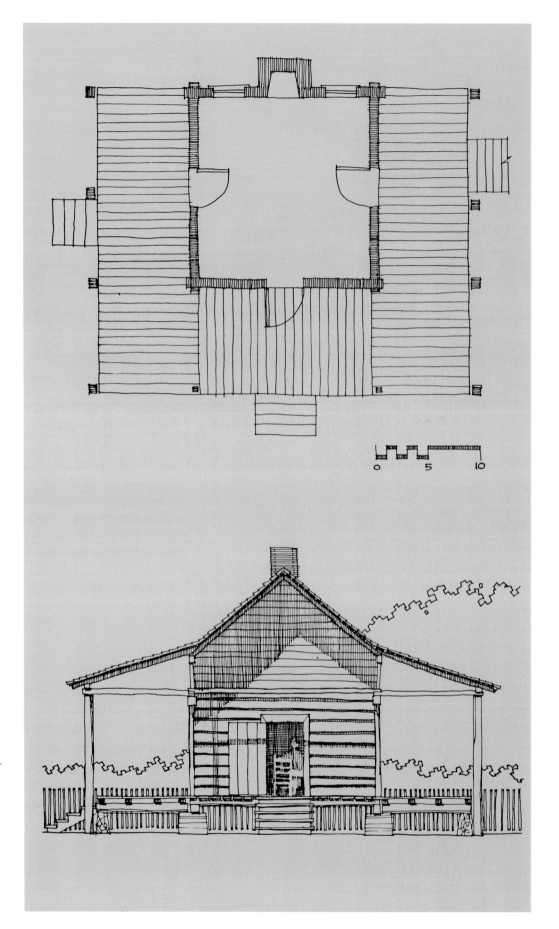

Plan and elevation of the McNair/Black House. The large porches surrounding the house kept it shaded in summer and provided extended work and living space for the family.

Interior views of the
McNair/Black House.

Above: Note the thick
clay lining of the fire-
place, round pine rafters
supporting attic floor-
boards, and a quilting
frame hanging from these
rafters, ready to be low-
ered in order to work on it.

Left: Note the large over-
head loom and the bed
and crib in the corner.

century depicts these backwoods settlers as dry, introverted, suspicious and fairly pitiful in appearance.

One such delightful journal was written by Iza Duffus Hardy as a collection of sketches on Florida life in 1887 and titled *Oranges and Alligators*. Mr. Hardy describes an encounter with a Florida Cracker as follows:

"Once we met an old man — originally white, but sunburnt to more than mulatto brown, in faded blue flannel shirt, with no coat, but in the stead thereof a blanket — (in urgent need of being sent to the laundry) — pinned round his shoulders with a skewer, a huge straw hat with half the brim divorced from the crown, an ancient-fashioned gun in one hand, and in the other the spoils of the chase, a coon and two grey squirrels, which he was offering for sale."

Mr. Hardy goes on to remark that while "shiftless," the Crackers, he had been told, were "a kindly and good-natured people, to whose simple hospitality the weary and belated traveler will never appeal in vain."

Another observer of early Florida days, Edward King, describes the Crackers as a "soft-voiced, easy-going, childlike kind of folk, quick to anger, vindictive when their rage is protracted and becomes a feud; and generous and noble in their rough hospitality. But they live the most undesirable of lives, and surrounded by every facility for a luxurious existence, subsist on 'hog and hominy, and drink the meanest whiskey.'"

The Boyer cottage was built
in Spring Bayou, Tarpon
Springs in 1878 for the
honeymoon of Mary and
Joshua Boyer. According to
early histories of Tarpon
Springs, Mary named the
town after watching the
tarpon leaping in Spring
Bayou. The cottage was
never electrified but was
enlarged after 1900 with
three additions which were
removed for its interpretation
at Heritage Park.
(Pinellas County Historical
Society)

The day's work had been cleanly. Feet were not soiled. Mrs. Lantry padded about on bare soles with a hand basin of warm water from the black iron kettle on the hearth. Each took a turn at washing face and hands with the coarse washrag. Lantry and the boys undressed as far as their undersuits; stretched their toes, cramped from heavy home-made cowhide boots, before the fire. Lantry and his wife went into the adjoining room and between quilts into a large pine bed. The girls followed into the same room, taking a smaller bed at the other end. The boys were left, three to the one bed, in the main room of the cabin. They called luxuriously to their sisters, thrashing their cold feet under the covers.

"Py-tee! Marthy! We got the farr! You-all never figgered on the farr!"

Mrs. Lantry called wearily, "You boys shut your mouths now. The girls is warm as you."

The fire crackled. The light played jerkily over the high new rafters. The Lantrys were warm under thick hand pieced quilts. Mrs. Lantry snored thinly, like a cat. There was no other sound but the sputtering fat-wood.

From *South Moon Under*
by MARJORIE KINNAN RAWLINGS

Log dog-trot at the Forest Capital Museum in Perry, Taylor County.

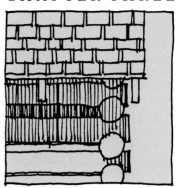

CHAPTER THREE

THE DOG-TROT
FOR A GROWING FAMILY

Now if we follow the progress over time of the determined family of Florida homesteaders introduced in the last chapter, we'd find that they had survived the summer floods and the winter freezes, the pesty onslaught of mosquitoes, no-see-ems and palmetto bugs, and the occasional encounter with brown bears and panthers, all of which shared these piney woods and hardwood forests with them. They survived and even prospered — not in any financial way that we might gauge prosperity by today — but their family grew, their crops matured and their livestock holdings multiplied. They might even have gained enough from some "cash crop," like Penny Baxter's little patch of tobacco described in Marjorie Kinnan Rawlings' novel *The Yearling*, to, now and then, acquire some store-bought yard goods for new curtains or the makings of a nice dress for wearing to Sunday meeting.

Raising crops, gardening, tending the land and the animals—all this communion with nature must have had a mellowing influence upon the likes of these originally gaunt, suspicious and introverted settlers. New neighbors forced a kind of sociability upon them as well. The number of homesteaders seeking to start new lives in Florida expanded significantly after the area became a U.S. Territory in 1822 and even more so with statehood in 1845.

But, if early Cracker homesteaders were begrudgingly helpful to their new neighbors, they were still exceptionally self-sufficient as they worked steadfastly to improve their homesteads by carving from the woods more space for planting and by adding one more room to the modest single-pen beginnings of their homes. More often than not this expansion was pushed to urgency by new little "corn crackers" popping up every year or so.

Expanding the homestead to hold a growing brood might have been approached in several ways. Adding another room to the original single-pen at the gable end away from the fireplace and perhaps even constructing a second fireplace of sticks and clay at the far gable of this new space constituted what cultural geographers would label a double-pen house. Two rooms, two front doors, a porch that now stretched the length of the two rooms and a chimney at either end. Add the new room to the gable end which held the fireplace and chimney and the new houseform was called a saddlebag.

Each of these expansion forms called for tedious reshaping of the abutted ends of log walls as new logs were interlocked with the original ones. Separating the new room from the old single-pen by an open space or breezeway was simpler, even quicker, despite the added log wall that needed to

be cut and notched. Good heart pine was abundant and more land needed to be cleared so one additional wall meant little in terms of material economy.

The result of such expansion then, more often than not, was the creation of the now classic dog-trot home, perhaps the single most recognizable Cracker house type known to us today.

One of the most beautiful examples of Cracker dog-trot construction is preserved for us at the Forest Capital State Museum in Perry. It was donated to the Florida Department of Natural Resources in 1972 by Grace H. Gibson, wife of State Senator L.P. Gibson. The impressive scale of the two high-ceilinged 17-foot-square rooms and the 12-foot-wide dog-trot between them give this vernacular structure a sophistication and a physical presence which is truly remarkable. The main house is constructed of square-hewn logs but the kitchen out back is of round logs, illustrating the progression in building technology described earlier.

For many Cracker homesteaders, the single-cell round log structure they had built to offer shelter that first year alone in the woods might very well have become the kitchen of an expanding compound of construction, the new square-log dog-trot forming a sizable addition as more living and sleeping space was needed.

But the construction of this addition would be technically different from that first constructed. The initial single cell had been built hastily in order to put a roof over the migrating settler's family as quickly as possible. Logs had been left round and simply saddle-notched to interlock with one another. No time had been allowed to let them "age" so that the natural moisture inside the wood may have led to warping, shrinking and even termite infestation as the logs slowly dried

out in place. From the legacy of living off the land and the tradition of one son learning from the experience of his father, such errors of expediency were corrected on the next go-round.

The logs for this new construction were cut in the spring when the sap was just beginning to flow. They were stripped of the bark that bugs and worms would otherwise furrow under and left to age in stacked piles until two seasons had passed. This time the logs would be hewn square using a pole ax to score the surface and a broad ax to strip away flat sections between the scores.

The Whiddon cabin, built in 1864, replaced an earlier structure destroyed by Confederate troops during the Civil War. This Cracker farmhouse is an excellent example of log dog-trot construction.

The Whiddon cabin was moved in 1972 from its original site off US Hwy. 98 in Taylor County and reconstructed at the Forest Capital Museum in Perry.

The notches that locked log corners into place were cut as "half dove tails," a fairly sophisticated wood cut that allowed all surfaces to slope toward the outside, shedding water and keeping the exposed joints dry. Since open end grain of these logs was most susceptible to decay, the best of pioneer log construction left the ends of the logs extended well beyond the notch to safeguard them against deterioration as long as possible and to permit trimming if rot did occur. When squared off at the notch, a detail preferred by some homesteaders, corner boards would neatly trim the house and protect the log ends from moisture. Broad overhangs at the eaves as well as at both gable ends of the roof did what they could to keep the logs protected from blowing rain.

Neighborliness became a necessity to the now more sociable Cracker house builder as the heavy logs had to be lifted high to be put in place and this took at least four strong men. Greased skid poles were leaned against the rising walls and, by pushing and pulling, each log was slid up the inclined ramp to its position. It took some knocking and banging to drop them down into closely nested contact with their counterparts in a tightly fitted dove-tail notch. The commitment to this extra effort as neighbor helped neighbor needs to be measured against the expectation that these new log structures could easily last several generations.

The kitchen out back of the main house is of round-log construction, saddle-notched.

The main house is of squared-log construction, with the logs sawed off just beyond the overlapping joint and the end grain protected by vertical corner boards.

It is interesting to note the ways in which these early Florida Crackers approached the building of their homes. They built out in the open, in a place cleared of any trees and underbrush, for fear that fire from frequent lightning strikes in the tall pine tops might wipe out their homesteading efforts and with it all their earthly possessions. Pine needles and any other debris were raked and swept away from around the house for the same reason. And no ivy or picturesque vine coverings draped over the Cracker homestead of yesteryear. These plants would have expelled moisture into the air, cut down air circulation and harbored insects that might nest or feed on the wood construction.

Additionally, and in contrast to Spanish colonial settlers on Florida's east coast who preferred dirt floors in their early homesteads, these inland Crackers, descendants from northern Europeans of Scotch-Irish stock, soon showed common preference to build high up off the damp ground on piers formed of wedge-shaped heart pine or cypress. Construction on large lime rock piers or stacked flat stones was occasionally employed as well.

Orientation to the sun, as these Celtic Crack-

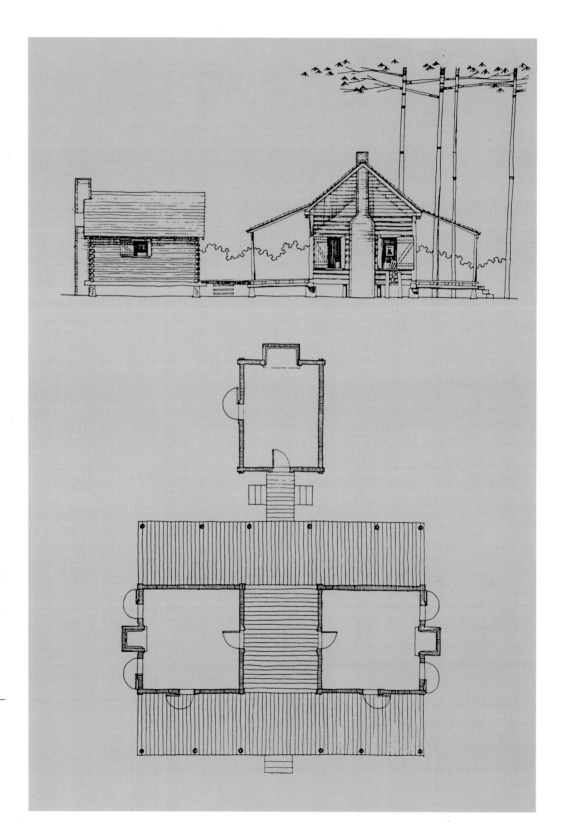

Side elevation of
Whiddon cabin. Note ex-
terior shutters on win-
dows and the wood pile
within easy reach
through opening.

Plan of Whiddon cabin.

Wall section through Whiddon kitchen, showing round-log construction. Details of round log construction, with simple saddle notching.

Wall section through Whiddon cabin, showing porch framing and square-hewn log construction. Detail of square-hewn log construction with dove-tail notching.

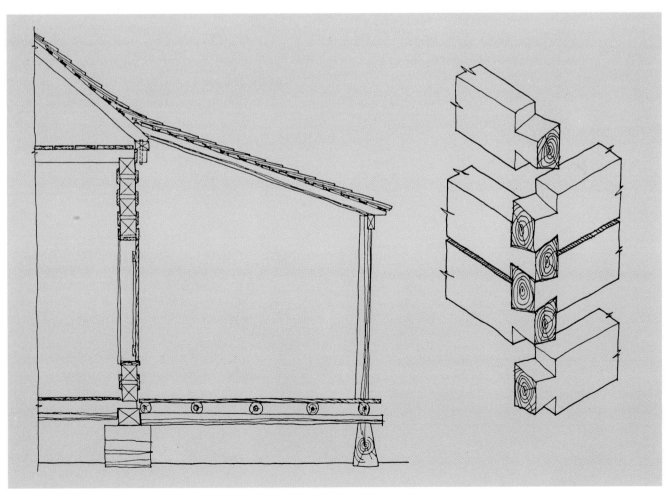

ers read the importance of this, ran contrary to contemporary thought. Today we would choose to orient the long axis of our Florida homes east and west so that a broad, windowed wall could face the southern sun. With this orientation we could enjoy free solar heat from a low sun in winter but be easily shaded from the high, hot summer sun by even a modest roof overhang. Cracker homesteaders by and large oriented their houses on a north-south axis. It appears that this 90-degree rotation from today's best thinking had to do with maximizing the solar impact on all three sunny sides: east, south and west. Such a tactic helped to keep the log walls dry. Moisture, leading to premature decay in wood, was the worst culprit in making a home unlivable. Placement of the fireplace and chimney in the north gable end would help keep that fourth sunless wall dry as well.

Finally, the construction of a pit or platform saw, where two workers cut together with the same long saw while on different levels, enabled the antebellum Florida homesteader to acquire thick-sawn planks for floorboards. In more developed communities, commercial sash-sawn lumber could be afforded, using water power or simple steam engines to run reciprocating saws. These boards would be laid over round log floor joists which were hewn flat on the top side and notched into the heavy sill logs that made the first course of the outer walls. Flat boards, sawn from logs as noted above or rived (split) from these logs, would serve as horizontal battening to seal off the space between logs. Wadding and chinking behind these horizontal battens with nearly anything available would help to shut out the weather.

Tied together by porches and overhangs, the homestead took on proud, dynamic proportions as the Cracker family settled in, satisfied and self-assured in its productive partnership with nature.

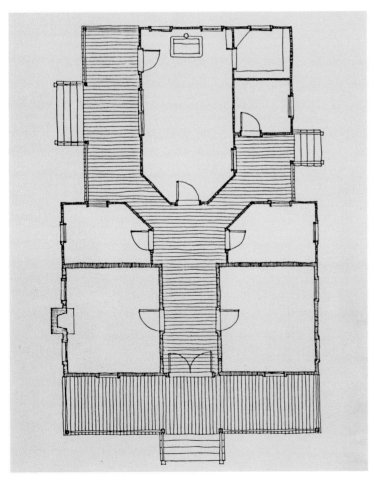

Exterior views of Old Settler's House: This later version of Florida dog-trot construction is preserved by the Manatee County Historical Commission. This beautiful frame vernacular farmhouse was built in 1912 by Will Stephens. Will and his wife, Roxie, had lived in a log dog-trot prior to this and raised five children in it. Their homesteading construction preferences attest to the popularity of the dog-trot houseform which continued well into the 20th century throughout much of agricultural Florida.

Exterior and interior
views of the Old Settler's
House in Bradenton,
Manatee County.
The parlor, kitchen and
small bedroom are
shown. Note the totally
wood interiors and the
traditional out back location of the kitchen.

Luke said, "In some parts o' Floridy, folkses makes a livin' outen cattle. Places where there's open flat-woods. And like I told you, heap o' the rich folks has orange groves. All around Windsor and Rochelle and Sawgress Landin they's orange groves. And cotton and cane. Folkses with plenty money raises all sich as that to sell."

From *Golden Apples*
by MARJORIE KINNAN RAWLINGS

Kanapaha, the Haile plantation house built in 1860, near Gainesville, Alachua County. A distinguished party of family and friends, circa 1905. (Courtesy of Mrs. J. Graham Haile)

CHAPTER FOUR

PLANTATIONS WITHOUT WHITE PILLARS

By the middle of the 19th century, the adventurous family-oriented pioneering home-steaders whose development we have been observing would have gained enough self-confidence from independently eeking out a living in the Florida scrub that they now set to planting fairly large acreages of citrus, cotton or tobacco with the sheer audacity that these might be money crops. As a test of their entrepreneurial skills, many early Florida farmers tried laying out a few rows of citrus started from wild saplings gathered in the cypress wetlands near their homesteads. Later they grafted them into the sweet and juicy fruit that the sandy peninsula would become famous for. With the Seminole Indian Wars at an end, a relaxed stability came to North Central Florida and many farmers were tempted to try tobacco, sugar cane or Sea Island cotton as cash-generating crops. The new railroads that cut across Florida offered a means to

An example of an I-house near Chiefland, Levy County.

Another I-house in Raiford, Union County.

get agricultural products to the coastal ports. From there the lucrative northern markets were accessible.

The family might now be two or even three generations strong and the farmhouse, which already had expanded from single-cell to double-cell or dog-trot, now needed to grow up as well as out.

In many cases, the open, breezy dog-trots were closed in to become central hallways and the makeshift ladders that reached to sleeping and storage lofts above gave way to permanent staircases leading to full second-story bedrooms. This new typological development in Florida, two rooms down and two rooms up flanking a central hall, resembled the ubiquitous "I-house" that was a popular farmhouse type throughout the east and on into the Midwestern expansion of the United States during the 19th century. Its simple, linear, bar-shaped plan gave it its referential name, although some would say that the "I-house" identification came from those states where it was most popular and whose names began with the letter "I" such as Indiana, Iowa and Illinois.

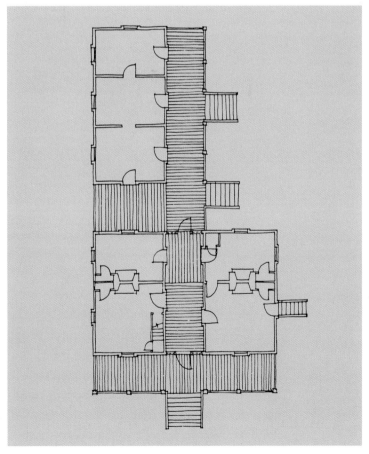

The Crosby House in Island Grove (Alachua County) is an excellent example of a transitional design between the early dog-trot plan and the much later four-square Georgian. (See Chapter 5 for discussion of this houseform). Built in 1885 by W.H. Dupree, the house was originally surrounded by 80 acres of citrus groves. Sold to George B. Crosby and his wife, Mattie, in 1903, the house was occupied by the Crosby family until 1976. (Photo by John Moran)

The dog-trot of the Crosby House is closed off with screening. The floor plan of this house suggests that the dog-trot precedent was on its way to becoming an I-house (two rooms wide, one room deep and two stories high) when a decision was made to move the fireplaces from the gable ends to the rear and to add two additional first-floor rooms in a shed expansion. (From student documentation project, University of Florida, by Gerald Brewington, Chuck Baxter, Sandra Horton and Julie Carlton)

The old Burnsed farmhouse near Macclenny, Baker County. The collapsing single-pen log structure to the right was built in 1889 by Mack Raulerson. He later added another log structure wrapped by porches and used the original single-pen as a kitchen. Harley Burnsed acquired the farm in 1923. It was abandoned in 1964.

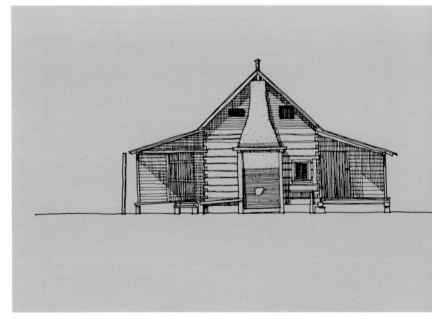

Families moving into North Central Florida at mid-century often built the dog-trot or its larger offspring, the I-house, as single full-blown pieces of construction rather than expanding to it through the early homesteader pattern of building a one-room cabin first. For the true Cracker family, however, many a single-cell log house

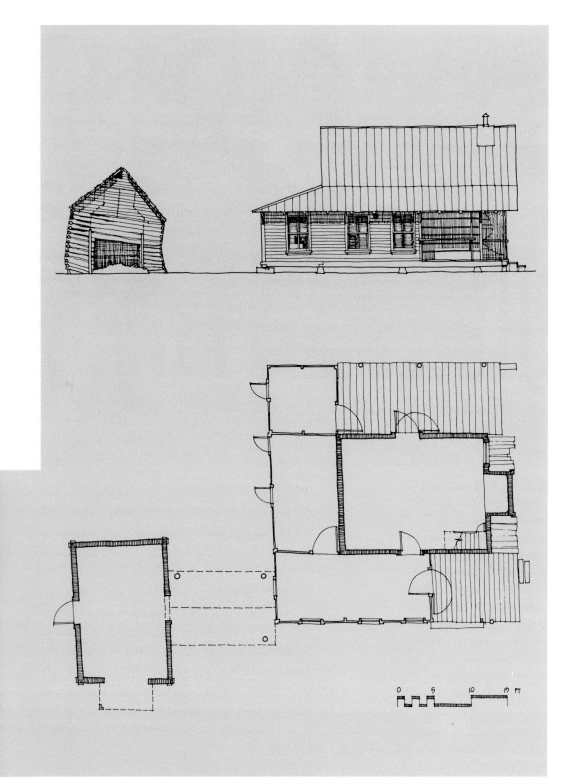

Plan and elevation of the Burnsed farmhouse. Note that the first (kitchen) structure was hastily built of round logs. The second (main house) has square-hewn logs. The porches on three sides have been partially filled in using clapboard siding for bedrooms, storage, etc. (From student documentation project, University of Florida, by Michael Clary, Keith Hunnicutt, Rhoda Lawrence and Michael Warren)

could be found buried under a board and batten covering and surrounded by a collection of added rooms built of braced-frame or balloon-frame construction. A casual ad hoc approach to planning seems to have pervaded house design in the mid-19th century as the family's need for space was attended to.

The Wardlaw-Smith mansion in Madison, Madison County. This antebellum mansion was designed in 1860 by architect William Hammerly using the Greek Revival style in favor throughout much of the South at that time. His client was Benjamin Wardlaw, a well-traveled political figure. Chandler Holmes Smith bought the mansion in 1871. The Smith family owned the house until 1978 when Mr. and Mrs. William Goza bought and restored it. The mansion is now a conference center for North Florida Junior College. It is interesting to note that as originally constructed the Wardlaw-Smith mansion had a second-floor balcony on all four sides, supported by square columns. In 1910 the Smith family had these simple columns and the balconies removed to replace them with 40-foot-tall fluted Doric columns. (Photo by John Moran)

As interest in the state grew, a good number of the newcomers to Florida in the years that immediately preceded the Civil War were experienced farmers — professionals, you might say — skilled and sophisticated in the art of making a living at labor-intensive agriculture. They moved into North Florida by the thousands, over 70,000 in fact, during the fifteen-year period from 1845 to 1860. Many brought slaves with them from their former homes in the Carolinas, the Virginias, and even states as far away as New York. These 30,000 blacks helped build homes, clear vast acreages of farm land and plant fields. This "plantation economy" forced many settler and squatter families off the lands they had cleared and built upon.

In 1842 Congress passed the Armed Occupation Act that encouraged white settlers to set up homesteads on large tracts of low-cost land with the intention that their vested interest there would lead them to act as citizen/soldiers and successfully suppress any further Indian uprising.

The plantation system led to the construction of many fine homes and a scale of building that the modest dog-trot or I-house had not foreshadowed. Yet the plantation Cracker was hardly aristocratic and no more educated than his homesteading neighbor. While he had wealth and an investment in perhaps as many as 100 or more "expensive" slaves, he probably could scarcely read or write. This lack of sophistication led to an architectural expression which was directly based

Left and below left: The Penelope Watkins House near Ft. White, Columbia County, which was later modified by the addition of a Greek Revival portico.

Below: A modest I-house near Lake City, Columbia County, which also was modified by the addition of a two-story portico.

upon tradition, remaining virtually unconcerned with the high fashion of other states. The Greek Revival style which had literally swept through the plantation society of Louisiana and Mississippi went unnoticed by the Florida Cracker regardless of his wealth or his status in the agricultural community. There were exceptions, of course,

Haile Plantation, Alachua County

Below: The porch floor and porch roof of the Haile Plantation are separately supported, a detail unique to few Florida homes.

as at Eden, the William Henry Wesley home in Walton County, and at the Wardlaw-Smith home in Madison, Florida.

Most of what passed for Greek Revival in Florida is self-conscious "dress-up." It often began with the simplicity of an I-house owned by a family whose newly gained economic success at farming led them to "gussy up" their otherwise austere homestead with fluted classic columns, two-story verandas and false entablatures — a kind of Cracker version of "keeping up with the Joneses."

Though the Cracker plantation house was true to the simple, unpretentious and unsophisticated social circumstance, it still remains strikingly beautiful. Austere and unadorned, like the Haile Plantation House in Alachua County, it proudly represents the best of the Florida vernacular tradition in this new construction type.

The scale of Haile Plantation is appropriate to the economic stature of the prosperous Carolinians who built it. Thomas and Esther Serena Chestnut Haile called their new home Kanapaha and built it around 1860 on a large tract of land bought with a sizable inheritance. Their relocation from Camden, South Carolina, was an adventure quite apart from that of the Florida homesteaders described earlier. (See p. 58.)

In 1985, the Haile Plantation House was successfully nominated to the National Register of Historic Places. The proposal read, in part:

The Haile Homestead is significant because it is an outstanding example of a large ante-bellum plantation house which has survived virtually unchanged since 1860. The classically symmetrical building, still owned by the Haile family, has never been modernized or altered. It is one of the few remaining homesteads built by Sea Island cotton planters in this part of Florida and bears a strong resemblance to early nineteenth century homes built in Camden, South Carolina, the original home of the Haile family. Commercial sawmills were in existence in many locations throughout North Florida by the time the Haile family built their new home. However, the large heart pine framing members used in this construction were all hand-hewn. Furthermore, the various beam-to-beam connections and the fitting of vertical wall studs to heavy timber sills were done by mortice and tenon. Wooden pegs, or trunnels (tree-nails), still hold each mortice and tenon joint tightly together.

Considering that over 300 slaves were brought with the three Haile families who moved south to Florida together and considering the sophisticated skills many of these slaves had acquired over time, it would be expected that much of the construction of the new plantation house would be labor-intensive rather than store-bought.

The hand-hewn diagonally braced heavy wood-frame structure is raised high up off the ground on limerock piers set in clay-lime mortar. Even the wood lathing that supports the plastered ceilings and walls was split by hand into irregularly shaped flat slats. The roof, which was originally covered with hand-split shingles secured with iron nails to wood purlins, is now galvanized metal.

Windows, doors, frames and shutters were commercially milled and of very fine quality. Porch and interior stair railings were assembled of simple milled sections and the flooring throughout consists of commercial tongue and groove boards.

The construction of porch roof supports at the Haile Plantation is of particular interest since the porch floor rests on its own stone piers independently of the porch roof posts. This anterior support detail was not uncommon in South Carolina and represents a transplanted vernacular expression that appears in several other historic north Florida houses. The Bailey House, 1854, the oldest existing residence in Gainesville, and the Asa May House (Rosewood), c. 1840, in Capps near Monticello are examples of Cracker plantation houses with anterior porch roof supports. Each is classically symmetrical in its plan and elevation and austerely beautiful. These modest, unadorned houses of wealthy Florida plantation owners represent the finest of frame vernacular or Cracker-style architecture of their era.

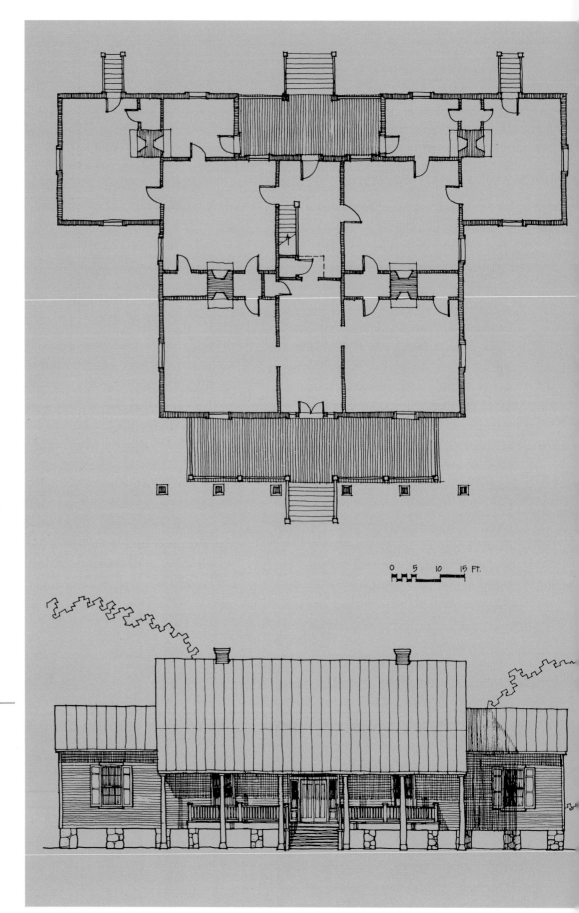

Haile Plantation House near Gainesville, Alachua County. Main floor plan and exterior elevations. The kitchen was in a separate building to the rear of the house. (From student documentation project, University of Florida by John Bellamy, Sergio Gonzalez, Jr., E.J. Marsh and G. Alan Urda)

0   5   10   15 FT.

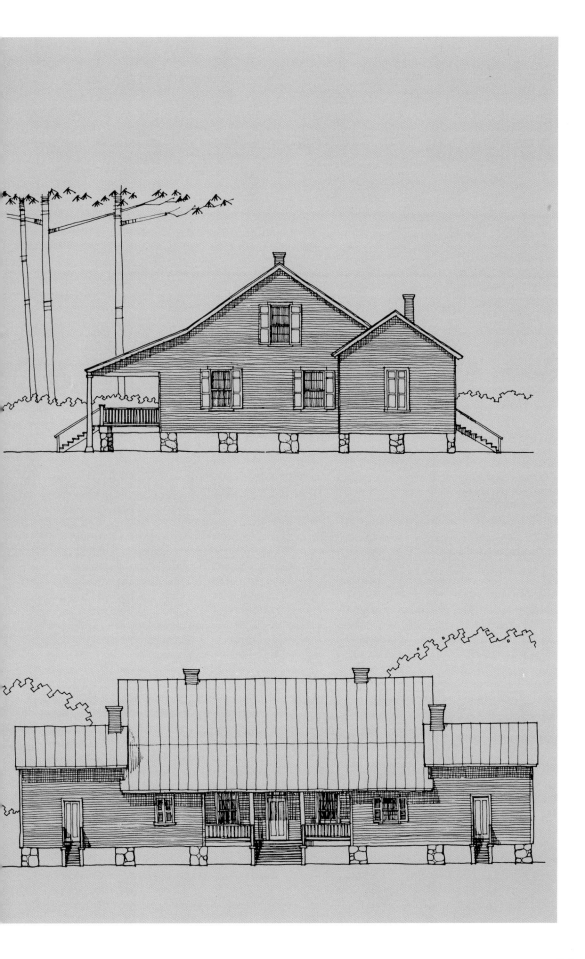

THE HAILE PLANTATION HOUSE

ALACHUA COUNTY, FLORIDA

The Thomas Evans Haile family immigrated from Camden, South Carolina, to Alachua County, Florida, about 1854 to establish a Sea Island cotton plantation; the spacious house, which they called "Kanapaha," was probably completed by 1860. Its porch with detached columns, the central doorway with its glazed transom and sidelights, and the classic symmetry of the design echo features which were part of the architectural tradition of antebellum Camden.

Family history indicates that after flooding ruined four successive cotton crops in South Carolina, Thomas Haile packed up his wife and five children and their slaves and traveled by wagon to Charleston, where he chartered a boat to Florida. Among the Haile slaves were experienced carpenters and cabinet makers and their skill is evidenced in the quality and finish of the Haile plantation house.

Alachua County, Florida, was on the threshold of prosperity when the Hailes moved to Kanapaha, an area eight miles southwest of Gainesville. Production of Sea Island cotton by settlers from Georgia and South Carolina had begun with the removal of the Indians and the opening of the Bellamy Road in 1826; by 1860 the Florida Railroad linked the area to coastal ports in Cedar Key and Fernandina, giving planters ready access to markets.

Thomas Haile was the fourth son of a prosperous Camden planter, Benjamin Haile, who had amassed a substantial fortune as the result of the discovery of gold on his property. Benjamin Haile's will, dated May, 1849, reveals that, in addition to 1,500 acres of land near Camden, Thomas inherited $4,000 in cash and an unspecified number of slaves from his father's estate. Thomas's wife, Esther Serena Chesnut Haile, also was descended from a prominent and wealthy Camden family. She was related to General James Chesnut, whose wife, Mary Boykin Chesnut, wrote *Diary From Dixie*.

The land the Hailes settled on in Alachua County was originally part of the Arredondo Grant and was purchased from Henry Marquand. Edward Haile (whose wife Mary was Serena Haile's sister), Thomas Chesnut (Serena Haile's brother), and Amelia Haile (Edward's and Thomas' mother), all purchased tracts of land in the Kanapaha area of Alachua County in the 1850s. The 1860 census indicates that each had a sizable plantation and owned numerous slaves (Thomas Haile, 66; Edward Haile, 101; and Amelia Haile, 175). It is likely, therefore, that the Haile-Chesnut clan, while adapting to the climate and frontier conditions of north central Florida, also du-plicated as much as possible the buildings and life style they had left behind in Camden, located in the rich cotton producing up-country of South Carolina.

Thomas and Serena Haile had five children when they moved to Florida; ten more were born at Kanapaha. The plantation house anticipated this increase for it was built to its present size by 1860, with four large rooms and two smaller ones on the first floor and on the second floor two even larger rooms used as bedrooms by the children. One downstairs room served as a school room. The kitchen, since burned to the ground, was a separate building to the rear of the house. Although the 1860 census indicates that the Hailes had built 18 cabins for their slaves, none of these have survived.

During the Civil War the Hailes, like most South Carolinians who had migrated to Florida, were staunch Confederates. Thomas E. Haile served as First Lieutenant with Col. John J. Dickison's Company H, Second Florida Cavalry; his oldest son John, who was in his teens, enlisted as a private. Their most memorable contact with the events of the war came in May of 1865, when Kanapaha sheltered Sid Winder and Francis Tench Tilghman, two of the men who escorted the Confederate Baggage and Treasure train containing the records and funds of the Confederate government. Tilghman's diary entry for May 23, 1865, the day after they learned of the capture of Jefferson Davis and the end of their hopes for the Confederacy, confides, "To day all has been confusion... we are all going to seek some point where we can be paroled and go home." Later in the day... "We were recd & treated very kindly by Mr. Haile indeed & a clean bed & entire undress after so many nights on the ground was elegant indeed."

After the war the Hailes continued to grow cotton. Many of their former slaves stayed on and it is likely that Thomas Haile expanded his production to meet the demands of a boom in cotton prices. However, in 1868, he was declared bankrupt by the court and most of his property was sold. Perhaps he, like many planters in Alachua County, had gambled on a big crop in 1867 but was ruined by exceptionally heavy spring rains and a plague of caterpillars in September. Fortunately, Edward Haile, who had developed a successful mercantile business in Gainesville, was able to reserve the forty acres upon which his brother's home stood. In 1873 this land and an additional seventy acres were conveyed by deed to Esther Serena Haile; these properties have remained in possession of direct descendents to the present date.

In 1979 the house was used in the filming of "Gal Young Un," based on a short story by Marjorie Kinnan Rawlings. The house was chosen as it closely fit Miss Rawlings' description of a large old house with "an air of prosperity," set deep in the woods.

Excerpt from nomination proposal to the National Register of Historic Places,
Prepared by MURRAY D. LAURIE

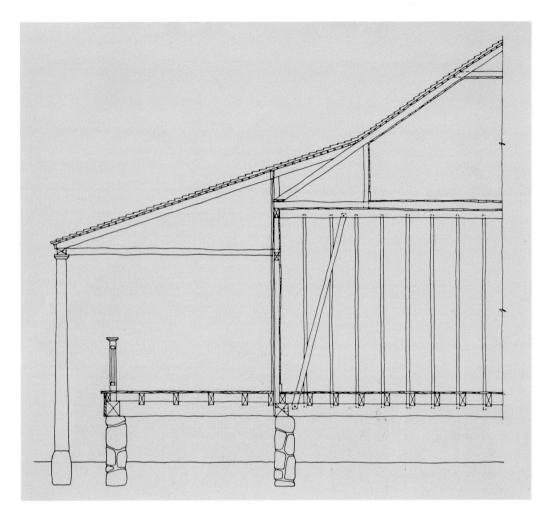

Diagram of braced-frame construction, similar to that used in the Haile Plantation House.

Kingsley Plantation House, Ft. George Island, Nassua County. It is the oldest plantation house in Florida. Built in 1817 by Zepheniah Kingsley, this wing-pavilion structure bears a strong resemblance to the north elevation of the Haile Plantation House, built some forty years later. (Photo by K. Tilford)

But in the towns and villages, . . . where neighbors were not far apart, men's minds and actions and property overlapped. There were intrusions on the individual spirit. There were friendliness and mutual help in time of trouble, true, but there were bickerings and watchfulness, one man suspicious of another.

From *The Yearling*
by MARJORIE KINNAN RAWLINGS

Four-square Georgian house, Madison County. (Photo by Dan Branch)

FOUR-SQUARE GEORGIAN
AND THE CRACKER TOWNHOUSE

About the turn of the century, Florida was emerging from its naive backwoods character into a fairly sophisticated but still rough-edged adolescence. Henry Plant and Henry Flagler were responsible for a good bit of this change as their railroads reached progressively further to the south and brought snowbirds and scoundrels in about equal numbers to this still environmentally pristine peninsula. The automobile and the truck brought improved roads, easier communications and sociability between farmers and merchants and replaced circuit riding preachers with "good-ol'-boy" politicians.

With improved access to the attractiveness of town living and the commercial activity there, many third- and fourth-generation Cracker boys and girls inevitably left the farm. They went to enter a new merchant class that not only sold the fruit of Florida's farmlands to Northern

While the Victorian era was late in influencing the mainstream of wood-frame vernacular architecture in Florida, the Donnelly House in Mount Dora, Lake County, was built in 1893.

Twin shotgun residences in Apalachicola, Franklin County.

markets but eventually the land itself.

Residential architecture in Florida had to change to accommodate the cultural sophistication of town living. The open, unabashed naiveté of the breezy dog-trot would certainly not do for the upwardly mobile town dweller. And while some highbrow college-educated agent for a Northern railroad company might put up for himself and his family a fairly stylish but informally composed Queen Anne pile, such interjections of foreign influence did not appeal to the humbler Cracker migrants into the same community.

Another new architectural phenomenon rejected by the white, rural Cracker was the simple shotgun houseform that had great appeal to black families moving into town, on their own for the first time. The shotgun house had a modest floor plan, laying out rooms and doors in a linear pattern from front porch to back porch. As the name shotgun implies, you could fire a round through the front door and out the back without hitting a thing. The movement from each room to the next was along one side of the house, without benefit of a hallway and without the privacy such features might provide.

The Queen Anne style that appealed to Northern transplants found its basic attraction in Victorian-era designs emanating from the international influence of the British Empire. In contrast, the humble shotgun can be traced back to African influences which traveled to the southeastern states by way of slave trade through the Caribbean

The Geiger residence in
Micanopy, Alachua County,
was built on the site of the
old East Florida Seminary in
1908. Structural timbers from
the former schoolhouse were
reused for sills in this four-
square Georgian residence.

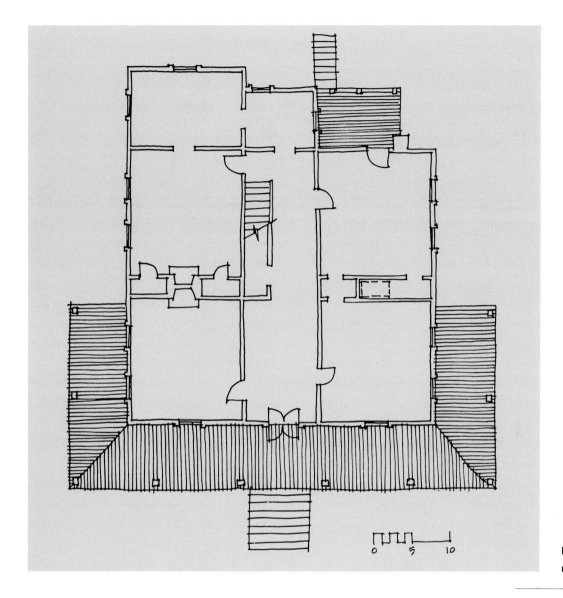

Plan of the Geiger
residence.

Islands. Its collision with high-style Greek Revival detailing makes it a curious presence in the post-Civil War urban South.

The physical isolation of the Central Florida peninsula permitted an escape from high fashion intrusions on the vernacular expression of its architecture for many decades. Florida's protected location out of the cultural mainstream of fickle stylistic fashion helped it to keep the traditional expression of its residential architecture fairly consistent over the dozen or so decades since the first Cracker pioneers crossed into the territory from the North and cleared land to build the single-cell

shelter described earlier.

Aspiring to move into town and join the mercantile or commercial shipping class, the off-spring of those early Cracker settlers initially found the shotgun house too modest for their aspirations and the Victorian decorative trappings, rambling floor plans and towering scale too pompous to suit their rural upbringing in the piney woods.

Belatedly however, the fussiness of Victorian imagery did win out in North Florida and the clear tradition of Cracker ways and imagery succumbed to it. Perhaps the last classic Cracker

FOUR-SQUARE GEORGIAN

houseform to have any eminence was the four-square Georgian type.

This new town-oriented houseform was kin to the basic Georgian or Federal-style house common throughout all the Eastern colonies. The uniqueness for Florida related to the use of impressively scaled pyramid-shaped roofs and to a tendency to surround the house with broad, shady verandas. The floor plan was classically Georgian, however. It consisted of a broad central hallway with two rooms to either side. These four rooms were typically large in size and square in proportion. Two back-to-back fireplaces and a common chimney separated each pair of rooms.

Out back, as with every preceding form of wood-frame vernacular housing in Florida, sat the kitchen. By now though, its isolation for heat and fire reasons would be modified by linking it directly to the main house. It might be noted that the tendency to clear the building site of tall trees had also been abandoned. The supplemental shade from oak or pine was a welcome feature in a passive cooling design strategy.

Life in town brought with it a new sense of territoriality for the Florida Cracker. In the open hammock, split rail fences had been used not so much to define property rights as to keep the free-roaming livestock from trampling or eating the family's vegetable garden. Such fences were simple and quickly built. They were not intended to deter visiting neighbors from giving a loud "whoop" as they approached the house and proceeded directly to the front porch to await the eventual acknowledgment that someone was here to sit a spell. Sociability was hard-learned over several generations in the scrub. It did emerge, however, albeit with an expected suspicion toward outright strangers, be they scruffy and homeless or snoopy and Yankee-like. A known neighbor was always welcome to sit or hunker awhile any time of day.

In town, the distinction between a family's property and that of new neighbors' was more hard-edged. There was precious little of it by comparison with a place in the scrub, and the Cracker town-transplant no doubt savored every inch of his town lot. Fences were now needed to define these new boundaries precisely. And while a rambling line of split rails or a few oiled posts with hog wire strung between might have been fine at the farm, such crude markers would no longer do to define one's new urban domain. Pickets were required: dense, obvious, sharp-pointed at the top and in a long repetitive rhythm that totally surrounded the lot. A gate allowed visitors to come in, if welcomed, but the new custom was to stand and talk briefly across the fence unless one was directly invited to step up to the porch and sit for a real visit.

Marjorie Kinnan Rawlings mused out loud for us in *Cross Creek* about how she considered replacing the hog wire mesh fence around her own house with white pickets. She wonders about the disruption such a move would be to the honeysuckle vines and how it might isolate her a bit from the orange groves. Finally, she decides, "the real objection is that an elegant fence would bring to the Creek a wanton orderliness that is out of place."

The porch itself took on new values for the in-town Cracker house. In the scrub it was a repository for those things frequently needed for either work or comfort. It was cluttered, convenient, a kind of extended "work shop" somewhere between barn and parlor. Now, in the town or village, it had to be kept neat. A rocker or two might be the only objects in evidence. Sitting and watching was a quickly learned social custom.

Split-rail fences commonly surrounded early Cracker farmhouses. This photo is of a residence near Newport, Wakulla County, built in 1903. (Courtesy Florida State Archives)

The picket fence distinguished the townhouse of Florida's late Cracker era, as in this setting in Fort Meade, Highlands County. (Courtesy Florida State Archives)

Clyde Sutton residence in
Micanopy, Alachua County.
This modest hall-and-parlor-
house type was later
modified by adding a
partition separating the
larger hall into a bedroom
and narrow central hallway.

Plan of Sutton residence.

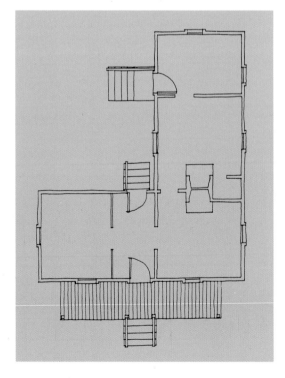

Being available for chance encounters with strolling neighbors was a necessary way to stay in touch with the news and gossip. Visits were now frequent and brief as opposed to the less gentle whooping welcome and long, deep visit of scrub folks.

Life was different, though just as genuine, in the new townhouse. Like nearly every other residential form that the Florida Crackers gravitated to and then passed on for next generations to emulate, the four-square Georgian was neatly symmetrical in both plan and elevation.

This is important to note. From the configuration of the simplest pioneering cabin, the single-pen house, down through its double-pen or dog-trot offspring, the homes of the Crackers had maintained a formal dignity. The ubiquitous I-house, the Cracker plantation house and, finally, the "late Cracker" four-square Georgian — in all these the classic principles of symmetry, formality and elegance can be seen at work. Only the hall-and-parlor-house type, with its inherent imbalance of large hall and smaller parlor, and the shotgun type, with its off-center entry and circulation pattern, defy this concentration on symmetry that Florida Crackers appear to have preferred.

It would not seem correct to ascribe this tendency for formal symmetry to some form of intellectual proclivity among these rough hewn pioneers and homesteaders. A rational selection process was, indeed, engaged in but it was not intellectual nor learned in the way that "high-style" choices were made. This latter form of decision making, based on one's knowledge of current fashion, was self-conscious, informed by data gathered from sophisticated sources like travel, social interchange and formal education. The basic

Cracker drew his information about architecture from none of these. His models were his father's and his grandfather's houses. His knowledge, honorable though it may be, was drawn from the tradition of one son learning from the observation of his father at work. It is particularly curious to find that this type of learning by direct observation and experience has generated, in the case of Florida Cracker architecture at least, a fairly consistent formalism that is beautifully classical.

We need to return to the definition of "vernacular" as presented earlier -- the native language or dialect of a particular region or place -- and use this as a measure of consistency in the minds and actions of those families who lived, worked and cultivated roots in the early settlement of this sandy peninsula. It is important to acknowledge this deep-rooted cultural tradition.

As more and more of their neighbors, both rural and in town, were true "outsiders" (newcomers, snowbirds and carpetbaggers) the Cracker offspring of the original settlers began to divide into two cultural camps. There were those who assimilated the cultural trappings of their new neighbors and went to work as agents of Northern entrepreneurs, sent their kids to college, and began to make high-style psuedo-intellectual choices on their own. In contrast, some held to the basic tenets of learning by tradition, employing handcrafts at home and labor-intensive blue collar work in either shop or field.

So divided, the descendants of the original Florida Crackers tend to be housed today in either the latest configuration of fashionable universalized taste or in the financially affordable modular or mobile housing units scattered densely throughout much of Florida's modern landscape.

The Earle Plantation
House near Lake Santa Fe
in Earleton, Alachua
County. Built just prior to
the Civil War, this elegant
four-square Georgian
home represents the fin-
est in classic Cracker architectural development.

Plan of Earle Plantation
House. (From field mea-
surements made by Kent
Cowherd, Frances
Hamilton, Arthur Kozik,
James Molinari and
Heather Talbert)

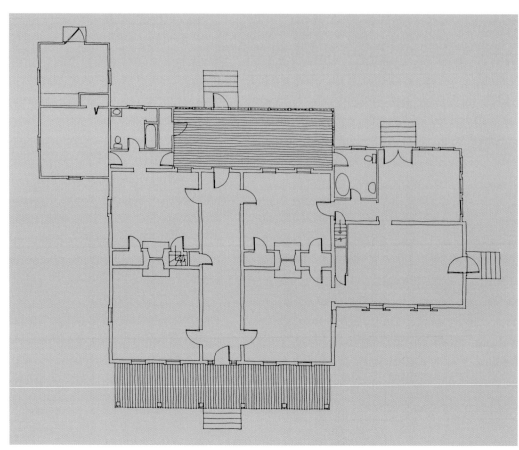

Elevation of Earle Plantation House. The louvered cupola induces cooling air movement through any open window or door making the house comfortable without central air conditioning.

It seemed to Piety that human habitation kept a house standing. Through the summer she saw Thad's and Martha's empty cabins sag a little at the corners, the roofs begin to cave in like battered hats. The rain pipes rusted through, so that the cisterns went stagnant, then dry. Oak snakes took up residence along the beams. The hammock crept in from one side and the scrub from the other. Wild grape vines began to lace themselves up the trellises where coral vines had been, and seedling pine trees sprang up between the steps. She saw with a strange clarity that it did not matter. Even Lantry did not matter, for her son walked long and brown across the clearing. The dead were the dead and the living were the living. The growing uncertainties of a daily existence absorbed her.

From *South Moon Under*
by MARJORIE KINNAN RAWLINGS

An abandoned and
dilapidated Cracker
farmhouse near Mariana,
Jackson County.

CHAPTER SIX

HISTORIC ALLUSION
IN A POST-MODERN ERA

A respect for regionalism is of growing interest to architects in many parts of this country. That fact is the intended celebration of this book. There are particular places where this interest in historic precedent has always been alive. In some locations this was true right through the lean, clean years of the international Modernist Movement. The New England states make up the most obvious of staunch traditionalist settings, but there are others. Such continuity of visual expressions may come by way of a deep-rooted respect for the past that was born of generations of stable tenure in one particular region. In more recently "gentrified" neighborhoods, new ordinances may define and protect the architecture of a particular historic district. In either situation, the vernacular settings in many regions of our nation do receive the respect and preservation they deserve.

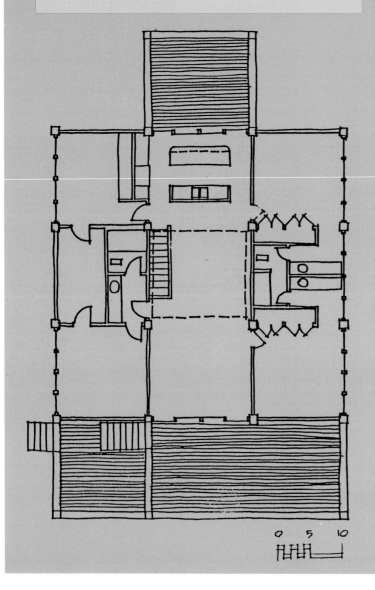

0 5 10

The typical dog-trot house of the North Florida Cracker was a two-room affair with a breezeway separating them but under a common roof. The Logan House, at 2,000 square feet, is understandably more complex than the Cracker precedent but it is still quite simple in plan.

The room layout is based on a grid creating nine squares or bays. The center three bays constitute the public spaces of the house: kitchen, dining and living rooms. These main areas serve the same function as the breezeway between the two rooms of the traditional dog-trot, that is, they provide an open space through which cooling breezes flow and they act as the family gathering area. By opening sliding glass doors at either end of this public hall, breezes can flow through unimpeded by interior walls. Bedrooms and a sewing room occupy the outside corners of the house.

Several elements not usually associated with the early settler's dog-trot house were used to good advantage: the tin roof and the cupola. The tin roof helps to deflect the harsh rays of the sun instead of absorbing heat as would darker shingles. The cupola is perhaps the most important of techniques used in the design to enhance passive cooling. During the summer, warm air rises up through the cupola, drawing replacement air in from below and creating a cooling evaporative effect.

The Logan residence has taken the most admirable qualities of the traditional dog-trot and enhanced them to make a very liveable and appropriate Florida house.

There are few of us who would not find great pleasure in visiting or abiding in such places. We seek them out. When we see the gray-shingled consistency of little Nantucket Island or travel through the stone farmhouse regions of Pennsylvania and New York's Hudson Valley we feel at home there even though our true home may be hundreds of miles away. We are refreshed and inspired by seeing the architectural consistency of Athens, Georgia, with its white Greek Revival houses or the pastel chromatics of manmade forms in Santa Fe, New Mexico. To blindly ignore such powerful historic precedent as we look for architectural inspiration is a form of heresy that is as incomprehensible as an act of treason toward a beloved homeland.

As to the regional qualities within the architectural traditions of North Florida, many designers have found inspiration here and have not been embarrassed by the use of such historic precedents. A few are illustrated in the pages which follow.

**Rowe Holmes Hammer
Russell, Architects —
Logan House in Tampa,
Hillsborough County.**

Each designer presented here deals with traditional vernacular geometry. Yet each attempts to bridge cultural differentiation as it has developed over the one hundred years or more that separate the original classic mannerisms of the 19th century from a more informal contemporary lifestyle. Issues of climatic adjustment through the use of ample shade and induced air movement are timeless, however. They apply today as much as yesterday, especially for the person who wishes to live comfortably close to nature in Florida. And, wood-frame technology seems to have altered so little since the Industrial Revolution brought us milled lumber and wire nails that new construction can sit compatibly next to old with little concern for being out of place or unseemly. Progress has been slow in the construction industry and the vernacular landscape is still quite prevalent throughout North Florida. We are all the better for this.

**Walter Chatham,
Architect — Ruskin
House at Seaside, Walton
County.**

*"The history of all architecture, including the
most modern, can be read in the simple indigenous
buildings which we so often overlook in our search for
architectural sources. The Cracker "shack" resembles a
variety of pure architectural types which are all
derived from the same essential source--the human
response to the need for practical shelter."*
— *Walter Chatman*

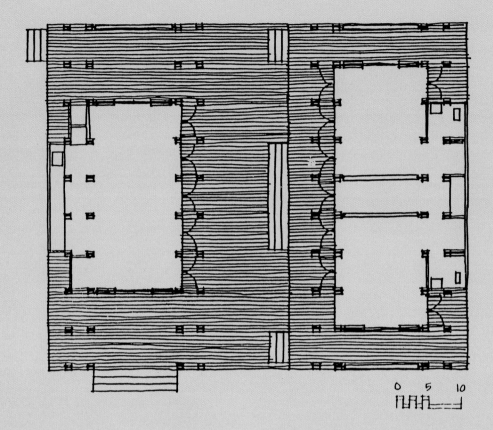

0 5 10

At first reading, the Ruskin House at Seaside is a more literal interpretation of the traditional dog-trot than Dwight Holmes' Logan House in Tampa. Yet its design takes a decidedly more radical approach as well. Architect Walter Chatham has, in effect, deconstructed the two-room dog-trot house of old and in its place provided two separate pavilions, one for living and one for sleeping. Both pavilions can be completely opened to provide maximum access to cooling ocean breezes, thereby limiting the necessity for air conditioning. The connecting deck becomes a setting where the everyday functions of living take place, just as with the original dog-trot when the porch served as an outdoor room for many different activities.

The house uses a noninsulated double roof system that consists of a metal gable over a metal barrel vault. The gable roof satisfies the architectural guidelines of the Seaside design code and, as such, establishes a strong visual reference to its classic vernacular roots. At the same time, the barrel vault and its flat-roofed side aisles serve up a provocative allusion to a popular Palladian motif without being trite.

From the street, the two pavilions present an aedicular image of Greek temples, very orderly and refined. In the open courtyard between the pavilions, the feeling is much more relaxed and unassuming. The pavilions seem to frame their own internal street scene.

The Ruskin House uses the design concepts of the traditional dog-trot to their fullest extent without resorting in any way to mindless reproduction of details.

Edward J. Seibert,
Architect — Vacation
house on La Costa
Island, Lee County.
(Photos by Von
Guttenberg)

This pragmatic little Florida house is reduced to the ultimate simplicity of its single-pen vernacular precedent. As such, it presents itself as an open umbrella of shade, maximizing natural ventilation and offering its protected occupants the closest possible link with nature.

Construction technology is appropriately simple as well. Pressure-treated round poles are set deeply into augered holes and standard lumber beams and rafters are all bolted together into a ruggedly wind-resistant seaside structure. Metal roofing is directly screwed down to exposed purlins.

"Both of these barrier island houses had to be designed in harmony with nature. Their passive qualities are very real, not theoretical. The concept of each is of a great wooden pavilion. Wonderful space, big porches — this is the special Florida feeling."
— Edward J. Seibert

Edward J. Seibert, Architect — MacDonald residence, Siesta Key, Sarasota County. (Photos by G. Wade Swicord)

In the spacious Siesta Key residence for author John D. MacDonald, the architect has applied the same directness of structural technology as in the earlier La Costa vacation house. Rugged pole supports are strapped to concrete piers in this case and the entire pavilion is raised high to catch the coastal breezes and to escape the brunt of hurricane storm surges.

Broad porches all around create a historic allusion to the vernacular precedent of early Florida homesteads. The imagined echo of clinking glasses and friendly laughter floating out onto coastal breezes belies the austerity of Cracker days gone by, but the spirit and honesty of this remarkable open pavilion is undeniably of this place, if of its own time.

Deborah Berke, Architect
— Gray residence at
Seaside, Walton County.

The Gray residence by Deborah Berke at Seaside is an excellent example of the adaptation of Florida vernacular principles to a contemporary home. The house is small at 1,098 square feet, but it provides the feeling of being much larger through its open plan. The rooms borrow spatially from one another as well as the surrounding porches. Its three-story height allows it to have a small footprint on the lot.

A stairwell acts as a thermal chimney. Warm air rising up and through the stairwell brings in cooler replacement air. The traditional form of the front porch is extended vertically as well, creating a street-side tower. This tower provides a sense of intimacy between house and street that at once welcomes guests while defining a semi-public or transitional space before entering the private living areas. The second-floor deck of the tower and a bridge connecting it to the main house provide a place to watch the sunset or the activity of the street below, much the same as the traditional front porch, although considerably more removed.

Details and construction techniques are reduced to their most basic form allowing the design to shine through in its purity. It is a house that most definitely has its roots in the small-town South, but goes beyond that to make its own mark in the world through thoughtful analysis and realignment of isolated elements and fragments more prosaically assembled in the traditional house.

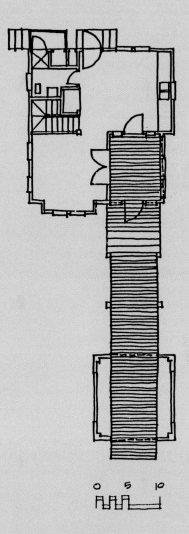

0   5   10

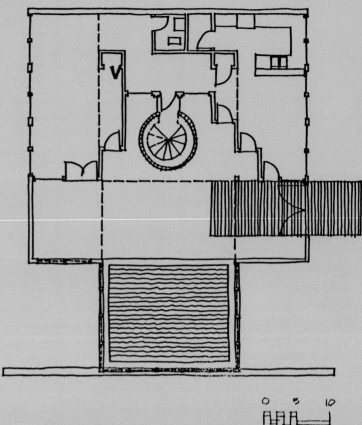

This last house to illustrate the concept of historic allusion being carried over into contemporary design is my own. It was the intention of this work to underscore several cultural ideas that gave shape to the Cracker architecture described in preceding chapters.

One of these ideas relates to the use of the porch as an extension of the internal volumes of the house. For two hundred years the deeply shaded front porch has been the place where the family could sit to do chores or to seek out a cooling breeze. As in this house, it was and still is the place to greet visitors or to lay out a table of food for celebrations with neighbors and friends. In effect, it provides a common meeting ground between the privacy of the family home behind it and the public qualities of the urban street beyond it.

Another cultural idea that is continued in this design is that of locating the staircase at a central and essentially formal position in the plan. Symmetry about this vertical circulation feature is a long-standing tradition within Florida's vernacular architecture and one that has been ignored only in recent decades. Space is balanced to either side of the central spiral staircase in this home, forming an intentional allusion to the historic I-house or the Georgian-style residence of the past.

A third idea drawn across time in this design is an effort made to reduce constructional detail to its basic essence. Nothing is adorned beyond its structural or functional requirement. This economy of means attempts to make visual reference to the same austerity which gave dignity and beauty to the Cracker precedent.

Beyond these points of identification with Florida's classic Cracker tradition, the aedicular form of the gridded screened structure over the small pool intends to reach even further back in time to the ancient symbol for house or temple. It represents, in effect, an attempt to restate the idea of Laugier's primitive hut.

"The technology of today is awesome, and along with keeping the pace and watching where we're going, it's important that we hold on to where we've been. That sense of consistency is crucial."
— Ron Haase

**Ronald W. Haase, Architect
— Haase House in
Gainesville, Alachua County.**

The gray of the house was overlaid with the tenderness of the April sun. The walls were washed with its thin gold. The ferns and lichens of the shingled roof were shot through with light, and the wren's nest under the eaves was luminous. The striped cat sprawled flattened on the rear stoop, exposing his belly to the soft warmth.

From *Gal Young Un*
by MARJORIE KINNAN RAWLINGS

An old dog-trot cabin on Lake Kerr in the Ocala National Forest, Marion County. (Photo courtesy Florida State Archives)

CHAPTER SEVEN

THINKING TYPOLOGICALLY

The vernacular tradition in nearly all regions and all cultures presents a strong geometric cohesiveness between internal space and external form. The visual vocabulary which links space and form can be surveyed and then graphically coded. The typological geometry that makes up this vocabulary is a key to the vernacular language or "dialect" of any particular region or place. Such a language has deep roots. It most likely evolved over many decades if not centuries and, as such, it has deep structural meaning to the very culture of such a place. The importance of this time-honored tradition demands the respect of each ensuing generation.

For the contemporary designer, surveying, coding and applying the regional vocabulary as described above might be referred to as "thinking typologically." It is a design process very

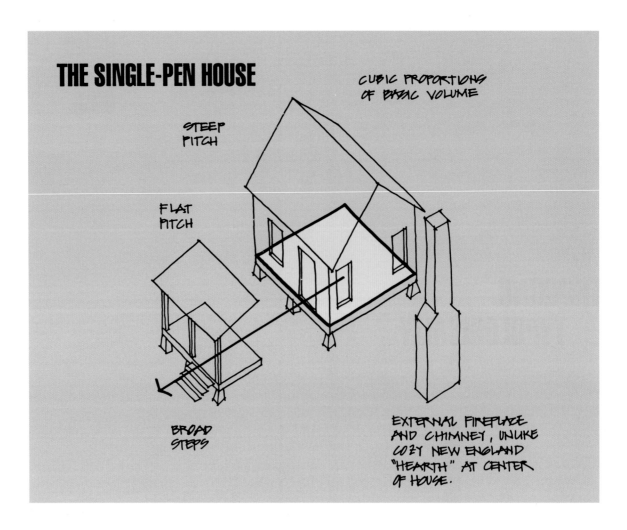

THE SINGLE-PEN HOUSE

CUBIC PROPORTIONS OF BASIC VOLUME

STEEP PITCH

FLAT PITCH

BROAD STEPS

EXTERNAL FIREPLACE AND CHIMNEY, UNLIKE COZY NEW ENGLAND "HEARTH" AT CENTER OF HOUSE.

distinct from that advocated in the Modernist Movement during the early part of this century. The modernists demanded the artistic license to solve functional design problems in a totally open-ended manner. The precedents of history were discarded in search of a free and innovative design spirit.

What is advocated here is diametrically opposite to the modernist philosophy, a design attitude which is still part and parcel of most architectural education. To embrace the neo-traditional or typological attitude requires a certain humility on the part of the designer, not an easy task, given the esthetic superiority most architects have considered to be their birthright. Like Howard Roark, Ayn Rand's fictional architect-hero in her "objec-

tivist" novel, *The Fountainhead,* the modernist would rather destroy his or her creation than defile its purity through the application of historic precedent.

Yet, thinking typologically, as recommended here, places a challenge before the contemporary architect which is no less exciting than the modernist credo. What is more, it presents an opportunity for a return to a responsible role for the architect as keeper of cultural heritage. Since the time of Pericles it was the architect/sculptor as technician and artist who was relied upon to express in stone and timber the best of humanity's aspirations. Such a responsibility carries with it the need to identify with a long-standing tradition and not with just the self-centered inclination of

THE DOG-TROT HOUSE

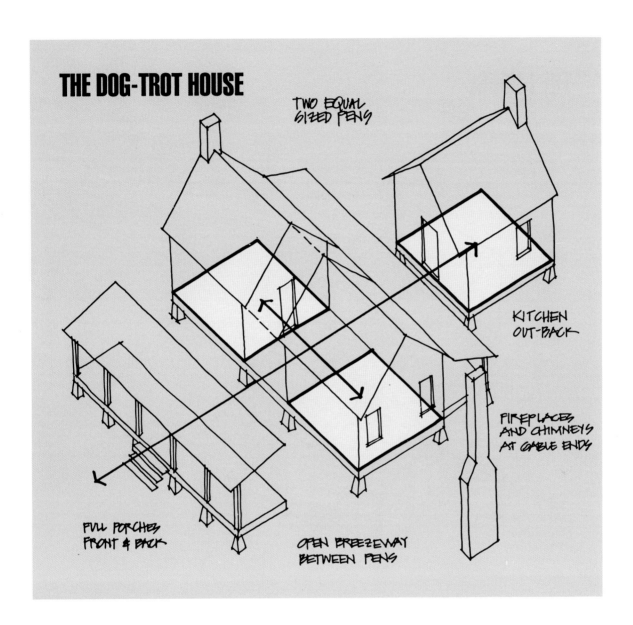

TWO EQUAL SIZED PENS

KITCHEN OUT-BACK

FIREPLACES AND CHIMNEYS AT GABLE ENDS

FULL PORCHES FRONT & BACK

OPEN BREEZEWAY BETWEEN PENS

the moment. In a time of rapid technological change, the necessity of sensing continuity across time and humanity's deep cultural identity with its past seems even more critical than it was two and a half thousand years ago.

Looking back on preceeding chapters, the typological evolution of Florida's Cracker architecture can easily be surveyed and coded into a readable set of images. As shown in the diagrams which follow, this imagery contains a vocabulary

THE I-HOUSE

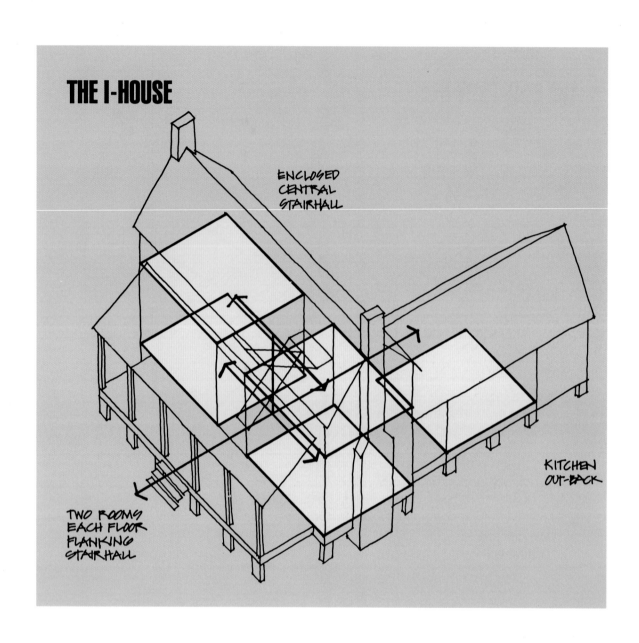

ENCLOSED
CENTRAL
STAIRHALL

KITCHEN
OUT-BACK

TWO ROOMS
EACH FLOOR
FLANKING
STAIRHALL

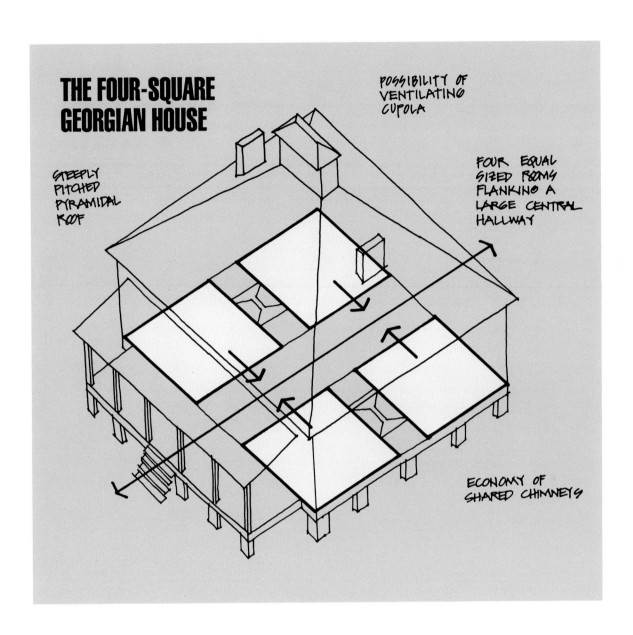

THE FOUR-SQUARE GEORGIAN HOUSE

POSSIBILITY OF VENTILATING CUPOLA

STEEPLY PITCHED PYRAMIDAL ROOF

FOUR EQUAL SIZED ROOMS FLANKING A LARGE CENTRAL HALLWAY

ECONOMY OF SHARED CHIMNEYS

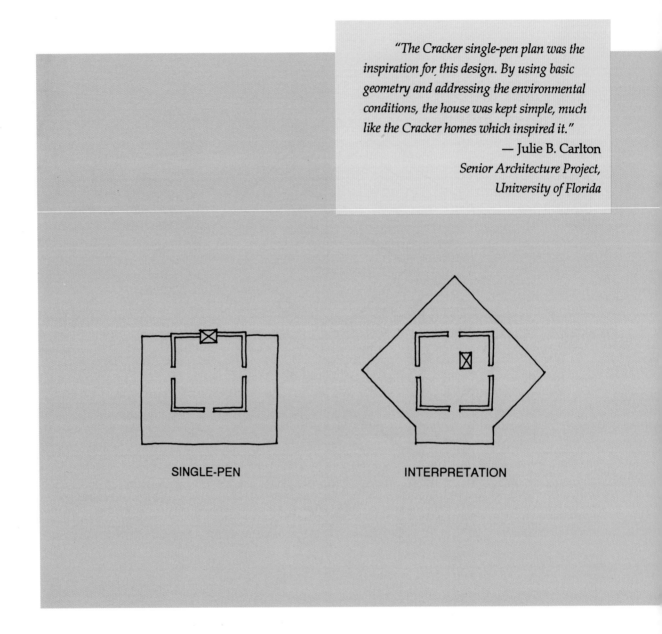

SINGLE-PEN   INTERPRETATION

of simple geometric forms for basic core elements and for subordinate or additive forms as well.

Engaging such a set of vernacular images into the process of thinking typologically requires accommodation of the design into a set of preconceived forms. Simultaneously the designer must be able to visualize both form and space, shifting them about in his or her mind until a certain logical fit begins to take place. It goes without saying that issues of site, context and economics also entered this visual equation as they do in all architec-tural considerations. But the important situation to be stressed here is that design decisions are being made within the limitations of a visual vocabulary which assures compatibility with a long-standing vernacular tradition. This tradition has been born out of an innate understanding of cultural, climatic and technological phenomena. To deny the tradition would be an insult to the very heritage which shaped this beautiful place called Florida and the setting for life and for nature that has continued over the centuries to draw us to it.

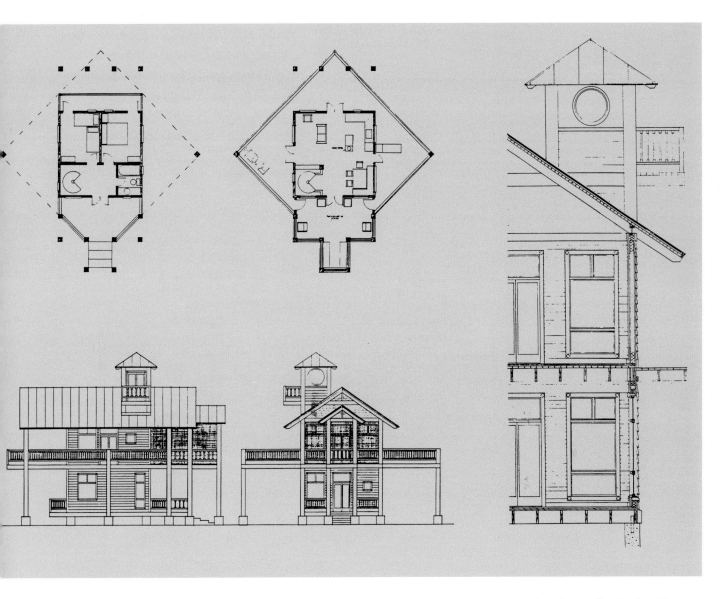

On this two-page spread and those that follow are some examples of how "thinking typologically" has worked for me and for my students at the University of Florida.

The illustrations of my own work were for private residential clients. The works of my students were done as projects in a senior design studio in the Department of Architecture. Diagrams on the left-hand pages are intended to identify the shifts involved in moving from typological precedent to the specific design solution.

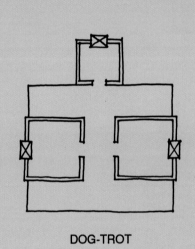

DOG-TROT

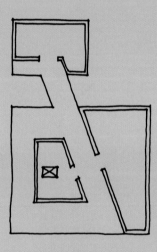

INTERPRETATION

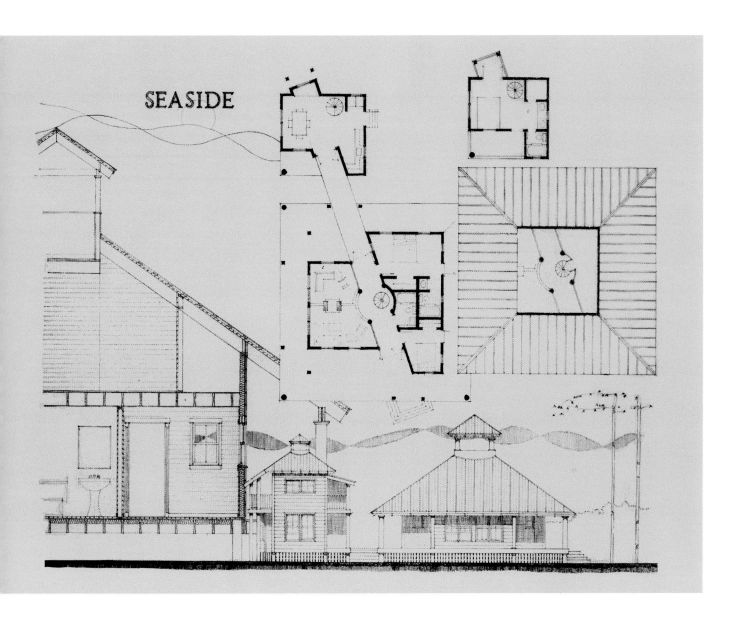

SEASIDE

**A student project for Seaside,
Walton County.**

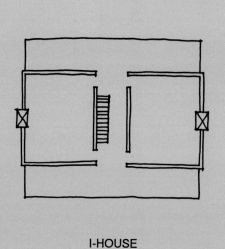

I-HOUSE

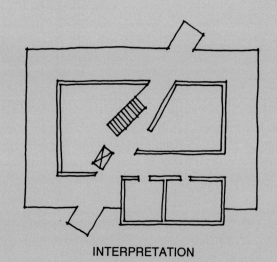

INTERPRETATION

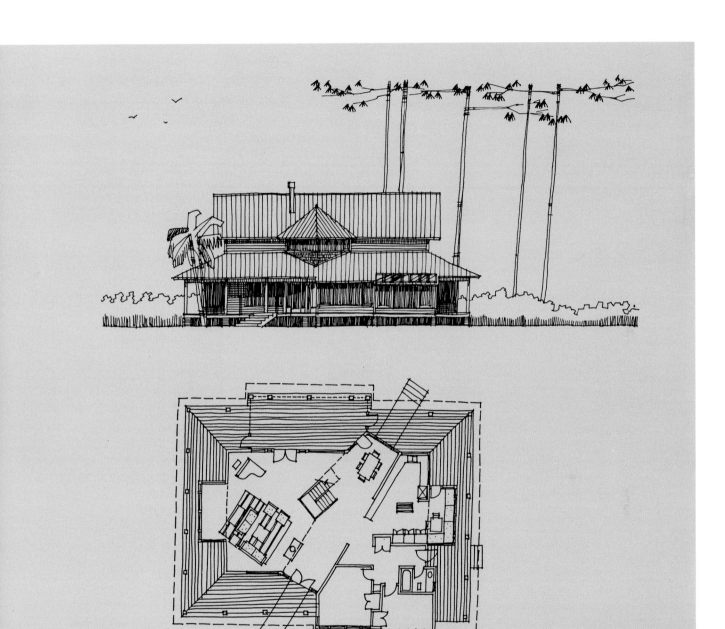

**A residence near Cross Creek,
Alachua County.**

SHOTGUN   INTERPRETATION

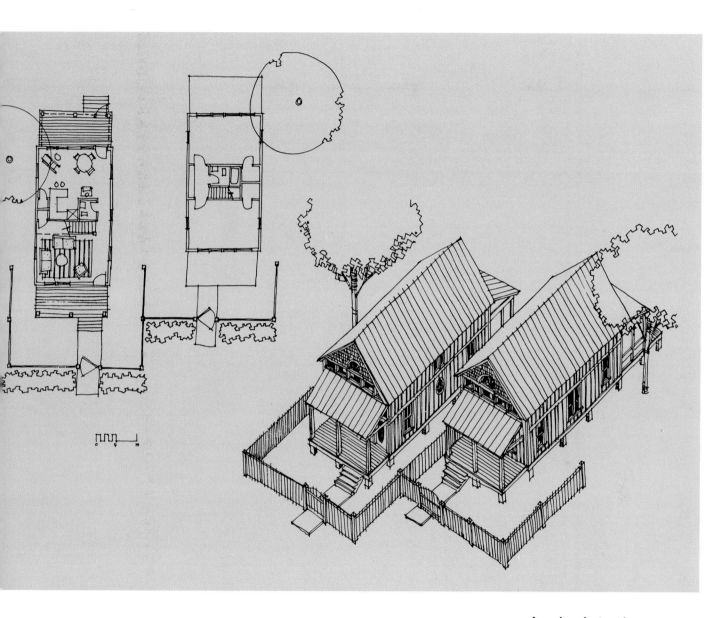

A week-end retreat in
Steinhatchee, Taylor County.

This contemporary Cracker house design suggests an evolution from the classic four-square Georgian type, with two rooms either side of a central stair hall, to a more functionally balanced and open plan based on today's lifestyle. Rather than four equal-sized rooms, the living room is made dominant in scale, rising up through the full two-story volume of the house. The kitchen becomes one of the smallest spaces, suggesting the efficiency of easy, casual food preparation. The pyramidal-shaped roof is retained as a strong visual recall of the historic precedent.

— Michael Hennes,
Senior Architecture Project,
University of Florida

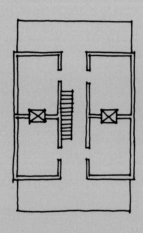

FOUR-SQUARE

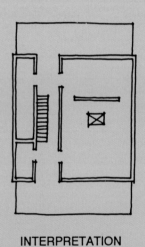

INTERPRETATION

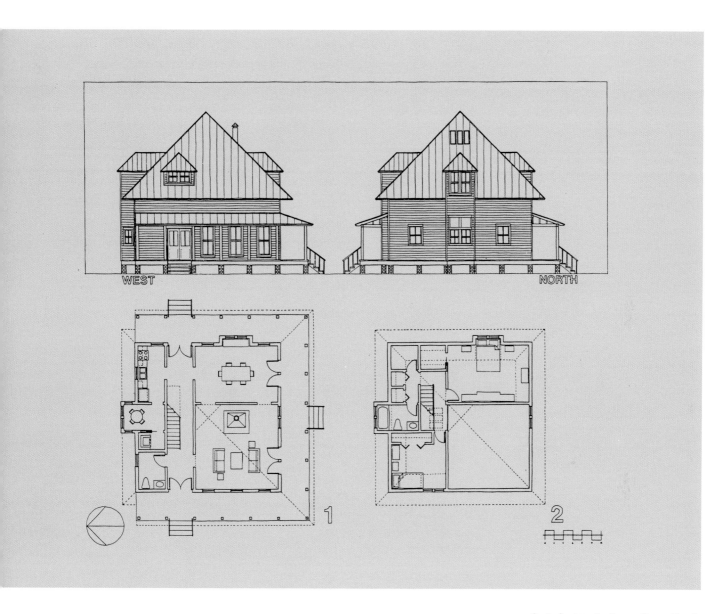

WEST

NORTH

1

2

A student project near Cross Creek, Alachua County.

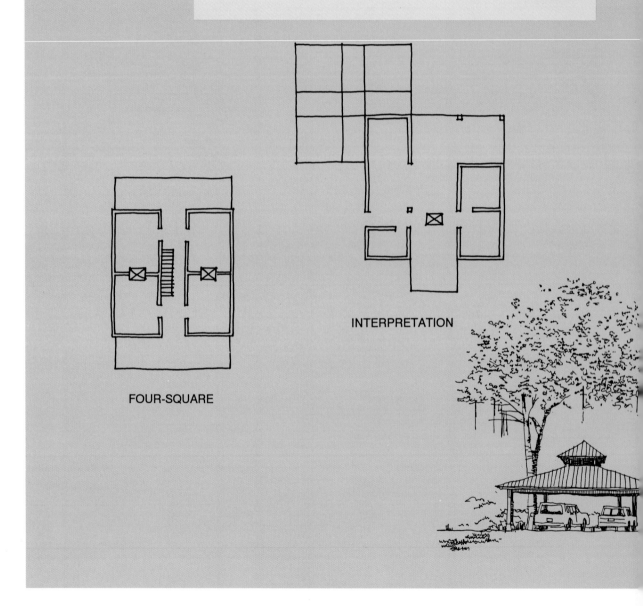

INTERPRETATION

FOUR-SQUARE

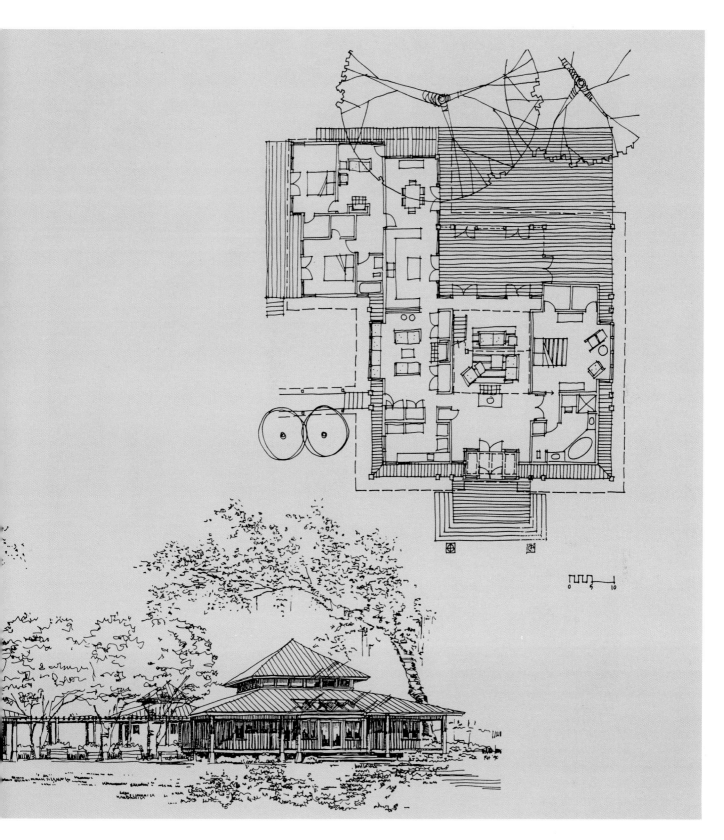

A residence near Micanopy,
Alachua County.

Old Joe lived alone in the old Mackay house . . . . The house is as silver gray as the speckled perch he sometimes catches. It is a tall box of a house and even in its desertion maintains a look of sturdy livability. It was a good house in its day. Something about it is beautiful, its color most of all, and tall palms bend over it, and there are live oaks and holly and a few orange trees around it, and the hammock is a soft curtain beyond it.

From *Cross Creek,*
by MARJORIE KINNAN RAWLINGS

An abandoned house in
Altha, Calhoun County.

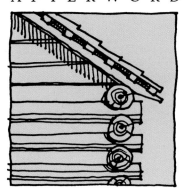

AFTERWORD

The design approach advocated in these pages is one focused on the richness of identifiable regional qualities. As stated earlier, such an approach involves a respect for the cultural and visual tradition in a particular region, an understanding of the climate there so as to properly enjoy it or to mitigate against it when necessary, and the pursuit of appropriate technologies expressed through native materials and the configuring of authentic detailing.

This collective application of culture, climate and technology as regional design parameters should lead to an architecture which speaks the essential visual language or dialect of the region.

As with verbal languages, this visual language is something that can be learned or acquired. A respectful visitor to another country would attempt to learn something of the native language there. It would be critical to social communications. Beyond the brief vacation where

An I-house resting in an open field just outside Webster, Sumter County.

such communications are awkwardly limited to the essentials of finding one's way in a strange new place, any long-term visitor would surely wish to acquire the sonorous characteristics, the regional dialect, of this host country. Of course it would be best to do so without being affectatious and without any attempt to hide or obfuscate one's own regional origins.

Here, in fact, lies the hard question: How do we engage in a meaningful pursuit of honest regional architectural expression and still be true to everything else we are heir to? We know too much. We are too sophisticated on an international level to fix our minds comfortably on such a narrow issue as regional architectural expression. Or so we have been led to believe.

The truth may be that we are too spoiled by the permissiveness of our self-appointed role as free spirits in the design world, or, perhaps we are still too envious of such freedom as it has long been claimed by other artists.

All art is social, however, and architecture is the most social of all. The responsible practice of architecture leads one to embrace society, to strive for an architecture which is readable by the vast majority of the public, an architecture with meaning that is translatable into the native language of those observing and using it.

There is no room for inside jokes in such a reading, no narrow attention to the focused gaze of an elitist few. Architecture is far too fundamental for this. It is the essential habitat of man. A certain humility is required in the rational construction of such a setting.

For some this regionalist design position may seem too delimiting, not very innovative, not flamboyant enough. I don't deny that. There should be great joy in the practice of architecture. As a teacher, I know that I should be urging you, the readers, as I would my own students, to open your minds. But I would have to ask you first to open your eyes, to look at the beauty in the lovely fabric of things around you, things already built and in place long before your personal act of building. I would ask you to reach out for the thread of continuity in all these things and to weave them back into your own creations with love, with respect, and with the most human of all characteristics, faith.

Such a regional approach to architecture requires that we understand the potential in historic "allusion" and how this idea differs significantly from that of historic "illusion." Illusion, after all, is mere copy, often shallow and only skin deep. As such it presents itself at a mockery of its historic precedent. Historic allusion, on the other hand, digs deeper into the essential meaning of the precedent. It is more critical in its response and more open-ended in its interpretation. It takes the form of a metaphor heightening our awareness of its relationship to the original. By doing so, we link history to the present and build a bridge of continuity across time.

There is one final recommendation with which I would like to end these pages. It is to suggest that each of us, from time to time, step outside our increasingly thermos-bottle-like air-conditioned offices and homes and drive the back roads of North Florida to Macclenny or Brooker on State Road 231 or to little Lloyds just off Interstate I-10 east of Tallahassee. Drive out along US 27 north of Mayo and, with your camera or your mind's eye, study the beauty that you will find there in the form of gently sagging roofs and decomposing verandas that make up the last of our Cracker Florida heritage. It will all soon be gone.

Shady porch on an antebellum log farmhouse near the Georgia border, Baker County.

Vacant house in Bevilles
Corner, Sumter County.

A listing old Cracker log
home near LaCrosse,
Alachua County.

**Enjoying a setting along
the Suwannee River.
Photo taken February 4,
1895. (Courtesy Florida
State Archives)**

Daniel Stoutamire farm near Ochlockonee River, circa 1890, Liberty County. (Courtesy Florida State Archives)

Cracker cabin built in 1882, Polk County. (Courtesy Florida State Archives)

Old Cracker farmhouse,
still occupied, in Leonards,
Calhoun County.

Pavillion style I-house in
Bevilles Corner, Sumter
County.

Single-pen log house in
northern Baker County,
collapsing at last after
130 years.

SUGGESTED READING

There are not many printed resources available on Cracker architecture. There are a number of excellent readings, however, on various aspects of Cracker times and ways and on the broader topic of vernacular architecture. The following have been of particular interest to the author.

Andrews, Allen H., *A Yank Pioneer in Florida*. Jacksonville, Florida: Douglas Printing Co., Inc., 1950.

Bell, Emily Lagow. *My Pioneer Days in Florida, 1876 - 1898*. Miami, Florida: McMurray Printing Co., Inc., 1928.

Dowling, Cassie Page. *Stories Told by Julia*. Dade City, Florida: Pasco County Historical Society, 1987.

Drake, W. Magruder and Robert R. Jones. *The Great South*. Baton Rouge, Louisiana: Louisiana State University Press, 1972.

Glassie, Henry. *Pattern in the Material Folk Culture of the Eastern United States*. Philadelphia: University of Pennsylvania Press, 1969.

_____. *Vernacular Architecture and Society*. Philadelphia: University of Pennsylvania Press, 1984.

_____ and Fred Kniffen. "Building in Wood in the Eastern United States." *Geographical Review*, 1966.

Hardy, Iza Duffus. *Oranges and Alligators: Sketches of South Florida Life*. London: Ward and Downey, 1887.

Jahoda, Glorida. *The Other Florida*. New York: Charles Scribner's Sons, 1967.

MacCauley, Clay. *The Seminole Indians of Florida*. Washington: U.S. Bureau of American Ethnology, 1887.

Matschatt, Cecile Hulse. *Suwanee River*. Athens: University of Georgia Press, 1980.

McWhiney, Grady. *Cracker Culture, Celtic Ways in the Old South*. Athens, Georgia: University of Georgia Press, 1988.

Paisley, Clifton. *The Red Hills of Florida, 1528 - 1865*. Athens, Georgia: University of Alabama Press, 1989.

Rogers, Benjamin F. "Florida Seen Through the Eyes of Ninetheenth Century Travellers." *Florida Historical Quarterly*, Vol. LXX, No. 1 (October 1955).

Smith, Patrick D. *A Land Remembered*. Sarasota, Florida: Pineapple Press, 1984.

Washington, Ray. *Cracker Florida*. Miami, Florida: Banyan Books, 1983.

Woodward, Richard. "Log-Cabin Legacy." *Fine Homebuilding* (April-May, 1983).

INDEX

Page numbers in bold italics refer to illustrations.